Acclaim
for
Butterfly Habits!

"Our lives are so busy we often forget how powerful the force of love can be in our lives. In *Butterfly Habits*, Fanny gives women a treasure chest of new and exciting things we can do to keep the romance flickering. No matter how you define success, this book will help you strengthen your relationship, the foundation you need to thrive. Thanks Fanny!"

～ Marcia Reynolds, PsyD., author of *Wander Woman: How High-Achieving Women Find Contentment and Direction*

"In my business I am in the midst of constant creativity and so it is difficult for someone to come in and surprise me with an idea. But that is what Fanny Ritter did when she asked me how I thought that a link between my professional skills and my love relationships could be created. The concept startled me at first and then I was keen to work with a woman who would come up with such a different perspective/approach to this topic. I believe that the biggest problem with relationships between a man and a woman today is that we no longer know what our roles are. So, as women, it is perhaps time to start looking at our careers and start implementing the rich, professional qualities of our professional skills into our personal lives and relationships. Any woman who recognizes this is an author on top of her game and worth reading. Good for you, Fanny Ritter!"

～ Holly Carinci, Founder & CEO of HollyWords Publicity Group

"The ability to commit, whether to love, friendship, or work, is a critical component of a fulfilling life. Fanny's words, exercises, and insights will help you make commitments with courage and confidence."

    ∾ Lois P. Frankel, Ph.D., New York Times Bestselling author of *Nice Girls Don't Get the Corner Office*

"Five stars for Fanny's book *Butterfly Habits!* Read it and receive a wealth of inspiration, keys, tips and pointers for keeping the delight factor going in your relationship."

    ∾ Dackeyia Q. Sterling, CEO/Publisher, Entertainment Power Players® (EPP)

"Fanny Ritter's own success in her personal life is evidence that these Butterfly Habits work and can be easily applied to your relationship. No matter where you are in your personal life, stop and read this inspirational book."

    ∾ Mark Shelmerdine, CEO, Susan Jeffers, LLC

"I am not always drawn into the 'plot' of a manuscript that I edit . . . with Fanny's manuscript I was not only editing but I was thinking and meditating on her contents. Fanny, I think you have great stuff. I like your voice, your humor but also the no nonsense way in which you convey your critical information."

    ∾ Dr. Tim Morrison, President, Write Choice Services, Inc.

"Healthy self-esteem is vital to a positive relationship. *Butterfly Habits!* will enlighten you with fresh ideas and insightful tools to expand your comfort zone and develop your relationship."

> ∽ Janice Davies, President of the International Council of Self-Esteem

"Fanny is such an inspiration to any woman trying to balance career and relationship. *Butterfly Habits!* is packed with relationship-changing advice and smart strategies that can start getting you back on track immediately. A great addition to your entrepreneurial bookshelf."

> ∽ Rosie Meleady, Awarded Entrepreneur and Founder of magazinecreationacademy.com

Butterfly Habits

Butterfly Habits

how to make your honeymoon last forever

FANNY RITTER MILZ

mpa

media press association

MEDIA PRESS ASSOCIATION
CH – 8000 Zürich
Switzerland
mediapressassociation.com

Ordering Information:
Quantity sales. Special discounts are available on quantity purchases by corporations, associations, and others. For details, contact the publisher at the address above.
Orders by trade bookstores and wholesalers. Please contact Lightning Source UK.

First Edition, 2014
ISBN 978-3-9524254-3-5

Print version by Lightning Source.

Cover design by Kathi Dunn, dunn-design.com
Interior design by Dorie McClelland, springbookdesign.com
Editing by Dr. Tim Morrison, writechoiceservices.com
Author photo by Fotiwoti, fotiwoti.ch

Disclaimer:
The author of this book does not dispense psychological advice or prescribe the use or any technique as a form of treatment for psychological, physical or medical problems without the advice of a physician, either directly or indirectly. Every effort has been made to make this book as complete and as accurate as possible. However, there may be mistakes, both typographical and in content. Therefore, this book should be used only as a general guide and not as the ultimate

*This book is dedicated to my wonderful husband, Urs,
and the loving memory of Eckhard.*

CONTENTS

ACKNOWLEDGMENTS

Without the significant contributions made by other people, this book would certainly not exist. I take this opportunity to express my profound gratitude and deep regards to the whole supporting team of John Eggen with special thanks to Christy Tryhus, Roxanne Gilgallon and Duanna Pang-Dokland for their exemplary guidance, monitoring, coaching and constant encouragement throughout the course of this book production. In the end, I believe that the team that was chosen provides the perfect blend of knowledge and skills that went into authoring this book. I thank Anita Wuethrich for her graphs, John Kremer for his insightful mentoring regarding the book title, Dorie McClelland of Spring Book Design for her meticulous interior design, and Hobie Hobart and Kathi Dunn from Dunn+Associates for devoting their time toward professional project management and cover design for this book. I was very fortunate to have the support and assistance of two critical readers and editors: Dr. Tim Morrison from Write Choice Services and Dr. Inge Treser. For their contribution and insights, I would like to thank Irina Countess of Plettenberg-Lenhausen, Holly Carinci, Tori Murden McClure, Rosie Meleady and Doris Hefti. They all reinforced my faith in the potential of the project and their interviews helped to make this book complete. I couldn't have done it without you.

I also want to express a deep sense of gratitude to my husband, Urs, for his cordial support, valuable information and guidance, which helped me in completing this book through various stages. Thank you, Urs, for standing beside me throughout my adventure and challenge in writing this book. You are my anchor.

Lastly, I thank my parents, sister, whole family and friends for their constant encouragement without which this book would not have been possible. Your feedback has been my inspiration and motivation for continuing to improve my work: Monika Castillo Diaz, Leticia Maria Conzalez Correas, Sandra Baker, Theresa Blanes, Sharon Bothma, Shona Cameron, Barbara del Amo, Sara Ferreras Somolinos, Susanne Forbes, Angeles Forteza, Beatrice and Kathja Gassmann, Sandra Gehrig, Cristina Gomez, Bente & Arnd Guertler, Silke Maria Haas, Reggie Harrison-Schelker, Kathleen Hilton, Carole Jean Rogers, Susan Joho, Bea Kaelin, Ulrike Kinzler-Straub, Caroline Luethi, Marie-Luce Legault, Silvia Mendoza Bisquerra, Claudia Munter, Hanne Niederbracht, Gabriela Niggli, Kitty Papp, Eunice Ritter, Uwe Reinsberg Wittig, Joern Galka, Monica Romero, Eva Ritter, Eunice Ritter, Jacqueline Speiser, Sabine Seifert, Ilka Yemanya Singendonk, Dackeyia Q. Sterling, Janet Tingwald, Dr. Richard Voegeli, Karen Yankovich, Mona Ziegler, Natalie Zimmermann.

FOREWORD

Fanny is an amazing personality: A fine, smart woman who moves mountains, stops the flow of time and keeps everything balanced . . . in a unique way! Her life story captured me immediately: A story for a novel. All about love, exclusively this!

For me, our acquaintance created the possibility to collaborate for this extraordinary book project, having awakened my curiosity . . . and grew into a friendship. This topic always touches and interests me, so I wanted to participate, to join the book at least with my thoughts.

I love people like Fanny. They are the sunshine in wintertime warming you despite clouds, rain or snow. They carry passion and love in their hearts, LOVE in capital letters.

And . . . love marks the beginning to everything, at least I feel this way! It unleashes the emotion of happiness and moves us in every direction, uniting the most different and sometimes even the highly impossible, especially in personal relationships. Love is the most powerful and precious energy in our life. The moment we lose it, we realize that love is the only thing that really matters. And love actually isn't a thing, it's a loving being. It needs care and is vulnerable. When I think of a loving person I remember a lot of little aspects about her or him, touching my heart. Each of all those aspects awakens and nourishes the magic of love in our daily life. Also, our own small habits are like facets of a precious diamond. Some may reflect the most beautiful part of our being and create love while others may be covered by a dusty grey. Fanny's book reveals the gorgeous beauty of the diamond, you already are. You will discover the essential facets nourishing your love, confidence and determination and you will learn how to give them high polish with smart Butterfly Habits. Fanny's stories and humor will enchant you, as they have with me. This is a gift of wisdom brought to light and guiding you straight to the core of a loving and fulfilled relationship. I believe that you will be fascinated, excited and very inspired by this extraordinary book. I want you to enjoy it!

Please be happy and make you and your loved ones happy. You can always find a reason to smile, a possibility for a spontaneous hug, a kiss or a small compliment. And remember: a face without any smile is just empty and naked.

Yours, Irina, Countess of Plettenberg-Lenhausen

INTRODUCTION

How may the habits of a butterfly influence your relationship's happiness?

The image has been shared throughout the world—the beat of a butterfly's wings in Brazil may generate a tornado in Texas.[1] Imagine: something as simple as the flutter of a butterfly's wing can generate dramatic changes throughout the world. And so it is with relationships. A seemingly simple, innocuous act or comment can endanger a relationship. Or it can strengthen the relationship immeasurably. And that is what this book is about.

I wrote this book to speak directly to women who seek to have an amazing, fulfilling life time relationship with their special man. What could be more precious than having a reliable man at your side who loves you deeply and truly? You readily share with him your dreams and visions. You feel blessed to wake up every morning with the loved one at your side. You are a model to the millions of women who reach out for this gift of finding the ideal partner. Would you be interested if I tell you through staying with this book for a while you can protect and conserve this precious love? Would you be curious if I tell you that some insights of a pro will keep you dreaming together although the years pass? Would you long to know how to preserve this magic attraction between the two of you?

Or, you may already be bonded or married for a number of years and be quite aware of the daily grind, which stifles your love's light so that you can hardly hear the melody of tenderness and romance in your relationship. Let me show you how to take control of the destiny of your relationship, how to transform arguing into true communication and how to convert the threat of drifting apart into an intimate connection of your hearts.

This book will not speak about rules because I dislike rules. They give a feeling of pressure and of having no choice. Often they set a frame that limits flexibility, creativity and growth. Strong relationships require flexibility, creativity and growth to remain successful for years! The word habit in the book's title refers to a specific way you act or react in daily situations and are driven by automatic behavior. Did you already notice the shift in your feelings about the perception of the two words rules and habits? Habits are completely under your personal control! Only you decide to align, change or eliminate them —whenever you want. Exclusively you have the power to make this happen. Habits are the ultimate key for handling the challenges of life and relationships smoothly and wisely. The information shared in *Butterfly Habits!* will not only have an impact in your personal life, but they will also have impact far beyond that.

You may ask: But isn't it hard work to change habits? Of course it will require persistency. BUT . . . and please take note of a bold BUT . . . the gratification will be immense! Your habits will determine if you can or will ever master a relationship successfully. That is certain. Being in control of your habits implies being in control of your relationship. A butterfly stands for transformation. The change from caterpillar to cocoon and then to butterfly doesn't happen by chance, instead the caterpillar's transformation happens through inner impulse and perseverance. The beauty and lightness of the transformed being is worth the endeavor. Therefore the title *Butterfly Habits!* speaks of the integration of unique skills to make you enjoy love and ease of a relationship.

You are the person whom you should value most. Even if you are concerned about the wellbeing of your beloved one(s), you need to stay the most important individual in your life. Your personal integrity is the most precious core of your self and must to be honored and respected at any moment. In alliance with that principle this book focuses primarily on you and later on your partner and relationship. Be prepared to slip out of the cocoon, pump up your wings and make your honeymoon last forever.

How to get the most out of this book?

Pick it up, start to read and don't stop until you have reached the end!

Even when I'm joking now, rest assured: the invested time will be worth its weight in gold. Nevertheless, I urge you to ignore that approach. Instead let me share with you what I believe is the best way to get the most out of this book.

It was March 2009 in Sitges, a little town at the sea near Barcelona in Spain. Dr. John Grinder, co-founder of neuro-linguistic programming with a worldwide reputation, and his wife, Dr. Carmen Bostic St. Claire, held a continuing education seminar on "International Certification in Coaching." The attendees were a mixed group of about eighty professionals: experienced physicians, teachers, therapists, consultants, coaches, business owners and executives. The first day after lunch when we re-entered the event room to our surprise all tables had been removed and the curtains of the large windows were closed. John and Carmen had eliminated all sources of distraction. The curtains covered the impressive view over the sea. Taking notes became a challenge since we no longer had tables. As experts of enhanced learning aptitude, John and Carmen wanted us to be fully present. I never will forget what happened then. Before starting the seminar everyone was required to leave the room, to keep all one knows or thinks to know about coaching outside the door and then to re-enter with the openness and curiosity of a child. This guaranteed the best outcome of the seminar.

My first recommendation on how to get most out of this book is to read it with a minimum of external distraction. Try to approach the stories and insights with the openness of a child's mind to win a whole new and unique perspective to enhance your relationship's quality.

Then, my second recommendation is as follows:

Shhh . . . don't wake the amygdala!

This quote refers to the book *One Small Step Can Change your Life* from Dr. Robert Maurer.[2] He reveals in an accessible language what holds us back when we encounter something new and how to overcome inner obstacles that keep us from changing. I won't burden you with neurological details. The only thing I recommend is to keep an eye on your amygdala. Your brain consists of three different layers. The first layer regulates the beat of your heart and your respiration. The second layer is the part of your brain responsible for alerting you immediately when danger threatens. The amygdala controls this second layer and evokes your emotions. The third layer and youngest part is your neural cortex. Whenever you want to approach something new the neural cortex analyzes the possibility of failure. And failure equals danger. A challenge evaluated as too big by your brain instantaneously triggers your amygdala. Robert Maurer indicates that there exist two ways people face this situation: they feel either excitement or fear. Most humans tend to act on fear. And fear sabotages the best intentions. How is this relevant to Butterfly Habits?

The book shares about seventy Butterfly Habits that will shift your personal perception and personality. You will be challenged to leave the old behind and reach out for new behavioral patterns. That process may activate your amygdala. Therefore, my second recommendation about how to get most out of this book is to keep in mind the power of small steps. When you are fascinated and inspired by the insights of this book, don't wake your amygdala! Instead of applying everything at once, choose one little habit and integrate it in a subtle way. Take your time and your journey to an extraordinary relationship will be smooth and smart.

As you read, you will discover that you didn't just buy a book. The contents expand beyond these pages. Through numerous cross-references to the website ButterflyHabits. com, the book offers you additional far-reaching and in-depth information. I shall share with you the tools to assist you in your exploration as you sharpen your perception and awareness. Never again will you be alone with your relationship challenges as you become connected to a supportive network.

My third recommendation about how to get most out of this book is: take advantage of all those free bonuses and extras.

Backstage of the Butterfly Habits phenomena

As a young girl I watched out for "the One" for me. When I won his heart, it didn't take a long time and I tried to "conquer" the next one. I enjoyed having butterflies in my tummy and was just playing until . . . Eckhard crossed my way. And, for the first time in life, I fought against falling in love seriously. Eckhard was twice as old as I, divorced and experienced: a man, not an amateur. Can you imagine that neither my parents nor my friends were happy about this relationship? I heard only: how long can this last? There is no future! He could be your father. This love was definitively out-of-the-box! For the first time in life I made a decision against all recommendations of the world. Instead, I listened to my heart and committed to our love. As a greenhorn in long-term relationships, I was fortunate to have Eckhard as a partner who grew from the mistakes of his first marriage to be a master of relationship. I learned the principles of an ever-lasting bond; and, despite all the pessimistic forecasts, our love grew and flourished.

After achieving my University Master's Degree in Economics and Social Sciences, we married; and the flow of life guided us to peaks and valleys. But all those exterior circumstances never affected our deep, true love. I was twenty-one years old when I met Eckhard the first time. It was twist of fate that providence took Eckhard's life twenty-one years later. Suddenly I was alone, my love lost, without dreams to live. At that point of life I was deeply convinced that I would never again share my love with another man. Why reach out for a stone, when I had held crystal in my hands?

But the most precious gift of life is love. It's an energy nobody can resist. So, magic happened—unexpected, and at first invisible. I didn't have the opportunity to isolate myself behind a wall or lift the shield of "ignoring." Love hit me a second time in life. How can it be possible that millions of women search their whole lives for the ideal partner while I got two? I am blessed. While Eckhard was an experienced master, Urs was a single in his heart, inexperienced in long-term relationships. Therefore, soon challenges surfaced in our partnership. Although we didn't always enjoy an easy "trip" together at that time, I always remembered the immense gratification of a loving relationship.

So, I committed to love, took Urs by the hand, and taught him the secrets of making the honeymoon last forever. Ten years have passed and we are both still in love with each other, enjoying a fulfilled marriage. Sharing life in all its facets with the one you love is the greatest gift ever. That's why I take *you* by the hand now . . . to reveal how to make your honeymoon last forever.

There is only one happiness in this life,
to love and be loved.

∽ George Sand, French novelist

Part One

Once upon a time . . .

Chapter 1

What happened to love?

One of the most challenging yet exciting decisions a woman takes in her life is when she says YES to marriage. This moment initiates a transformation of her life. Even if you have shared several years with your partner—it will not be the same any more. Your status in society shifts from Ms. to Mrs. and although this may seem a simple variation of one single letter its impact is great. It officially indicates that your heart is bonded with another and is no longer available.

When I got married the first time, it was usual to adopt your husband's name. In less than a day, my "single name" disappeared, vanished from my existence. Honestly that was a strange feeling, as my personality and existence were so deeply connected to my parents' name. At least, that's the way I felt. Deciding to become married truly changes a woman's existence. The day you enter the town hall or county court house to initiate your marriage marks a significant point in your life.

Let's take a journey with the time machine back to that special day when Eckhard, my first husband, and I announced our marriage at town hall many years ago. The responsible civil registrar immediately offered his congratulations to our decision with the best wishes for the common future. Then he informed us in detail how responsibilities, permissions and legal rights would shift and impact on our common life. As a next step, the official journal published our request for marriage for three weeks before the official ceremony took place. During that time anyone could offer arguments against our decision to get married.

Now, imagine switching twenty years later to the future: Urs and I entered town hall also with the intention to announce our marriage. The responsible civil registrar asked us to enter her office in order to register our personal data. Then the unbelievable happened. At this very special moment of commitment in Urs' and my life, she started to inform us in detail about the procedure of a divorce: when, where and how to initiate such a process. After awhile Urs interrupted her: We are here because we want to marry. Details about divorce are not of interest. The civil registrar, irritated by Urs' comment, explained that today it was common and that it was her obligation to inform couples about the divorce process, as the chance for a long-lasting marriage is small. Referring to this, she said that a marriage request didn't get published any more. Today's statistics reveal that this would only be a waste of time and money.

Imagine twenty years ahead from now: I am wondering what the official process of entering marriage will look like? Maybe we approach this special step in life like a hosting contract of a website. There would be the option to get married for one, three or five years with an automatic renewal unless the couple indicates otherwise. Or maybe marriage completely disappears, because we are unable to stand for this official one-to-one commitment, incapable of overcoming any arising challenge successfully? Will long-term romance vanish from human existence?

What the heck happened to love!

Chapter 2

Myths, illusions, and facts every woman needs to know

Learning is not attained by chance,
it must be sought for with ardor and diligence.

⌐ Abigail Adams, U.S. First Lady

A woman isn't taught the nature of a man and a man usually knows nothing about the essence of a woman. The consequences show up mercilessly in countless relationships.

We live in a transitional period as the role of woman and man in society and in relationships have profoundly changed. The model of the "ideal" partnership doesn't exist any more. You are part of the generation being challenged to have and to build a new vision of togetherness between woman and man. We all are called on to turn the page of ancient family structures and create spheres that offer respect for individuality and a loving coexistence equally. If we want to change the world, it's up to us to initiate transformations. Social and educational adjustments lie behind this change. So, we are lonely fighters in the greatest relationship revolution of all times. As a consequence, figures, statistics and surveys speak for themselves in absolute terms:

FACT #1

The $30 billion pain

Research determined that a single divorce costs state and federal governments about $30,000 and extrapolations of estimates reveal that divorce and its consequences cost the United States taxpayers about $30 billion annually.[3] The emphasis is on annually. Imagine the pain and suffering behind those bare figures! Do you hear a call for action? I did and that is what led me to write this book. Every woman, including you, needs to be aware of the bad ghosts threatening her relationship's love and happiness!

FACT #2

The "seven-year" itch persists

After decades of increases, U.S. divorces are leveling off with couples now slightly more likely to reach their 10-year wedding anniversary. But the "seven-year itch" among couples persists, with nearly 1 out of 2 first marriages estimated to end in divorce.

⤳ Huffington Post[4]

A sword of Damocles hovers menacingly over relationships. An impending divorce often roots in countless, subtle reasons most couples aren't even aware of. Unresolved disagreements and mutual misunderstandings mark the destiny of love like a drop of water falling on a stone. At the beginning nothing seems to happen, but in the course of time those drops can split the most solid rock. The "seven-year itch" still remains a milestone in a relationship. Be with this book and with me and discover how to avoid it.

FACT #3

Experience is useful, but does not always equal wisdom

For a child, learning to walk is a huge challenge: to gain strength in the legs, to balance the body in all conditions. How many times did you fall? Still, you knew that it was possible to achieve, and you tried, over and over again. Inspiration, motivation and persistence made you succeed. Unfortunately, statistics show that this principle doesn't necessarily apply in love relationships:

In America, the divorce rate for a first marriage is around 41%. The divorce rate for a second marriage is 60%. The divorce rate for a third marriage is 73%.[5]

In a radio interview I attended, the presenter—Thomas Skipwith—came up with an English saying: "You are not divorced? Then you have no experience in relationship issues." This phrase reflects the misconception that only a divorce can teach you to handle a partnership successfully. You do not have to crash your vehicle in order to be a savvy car driver! Other options definitely exist. *Butterfly Habits:*

How to Make Your Honeymoon Last Forever offers ambitious insights to prevent the "crashing" of your love.

FACT #4

Woman's war of love and career

Wife, mother, career: from the beginning women all over the world face challenges of life balance they never were educated or trained for. It is not surprising that this situation is also reflected in studies and surveys:

> I also find that the incidence in divorce is far higher in couples where both spouses are working than in couples where only one spouse is employed.[6]

As a relationship evolves, new understandings of one's role in the relationship emerge for both partners. But tradition makes it difficult to adapt. It is not surprising when studies reveal that women's work hours increase the risk of divorce while men's increasing work hours often show little statistical impact. To enjoy a personal as well as a professional life, today's woman is required to transform herself into a Top Manager. The smart principles and Butterfly Habits of this book will make you ensure long-term happiness in your love and life.

AND . . .

regardless of all those impending consequences a survey[7] reveals that 96% of college students who want to marry or are already married, agree with this statement:

Having close family relationships is a key to happiness.

Love is and stays an important issue in today's life. Also you were or are part of those 96%.

But bad ghosts do threaten the bond of every relationship. Maybe the love of you two is still strong enough to chase these ghosts away or maybe your relationship is already contaminated.

The bad ghost of commitment or . . .

The Myth of "Once committed, always committed"

Twenty-five years ago a book with blank pages became a worldwide best seller: Everything Men Know about Women by Dr. Alan Francis. The blank pages of this book may illustrate the emptiness you feel in your relationship. The brilliant colors of your love's canvas have faded and a monotonous gray dominates your life. When did you last hear the words I love you from your partner? Where is your Prince Charming today? Maybe you are still committed to your love, while he seems more committed to himself. Your inner voice starts whispering doubts, playing a damaged record of all the errors and mistakes he ever committed. Your partner's weaknesses grow to a giant size. You fight against this bad ghost inside your mind. But you know some of the arguments are true. All you have to do is look at what goes on each day (or what doesn't happen). Your resistance starts crumbling and the day comes when you ask yourself the ultimate question:

Is it worth it?

Have you ever broken a commitment? When you commit, you act on specific terms and conditions. Additionally you generate an expectation of the future. The same happens to your partner. Maybe the course of life evokes little discrepancies that start triggering slight feelings of discontent. But over time, as the discrepancies steadily increase, those feelings of unhappiness accumulate to a clear sense of dissatisfaction. Then the moment comes when commitment is called into question. What happened? Have some terms or conditions changed? Has the once anticipated future that has become the present arrived far different from the expected one? Has the romantic story of common love arrived at its end? Since nothing in the book of love is set in black and white, change reflects the nature of life. It's not about looking for a scapegoat. Sensitivity and openness are the keys to handle such a situation successfully; ignoring each other's feeling would only widen the gap. Many women appear to be blind about this natural process of a commitment. They keep following the illusion of "Once committed, always committed." Banish this illusion from your mind.

The bad ghost of disinterest or . . .

The illusion of "Only he changed"

When did the paths of your lives start drifting away from each other? He may live in a world to which you no longer have access. The door lock was replaced and your key doesn't fit. While you are longing for his love with all your senses, he doesn't listen any more. He simply doesn't understand what you want or wish. You seem to annoy him. When you recall the days of your "honeymoon," he gets upset and feels provoked. Once you shared your secret dreams and pains. Once he was your safe rock in the stormy days of your life. Now disinterest creates a growing vacuum in your relationship's love. A subtle thought starts generating a dangerous illusion.

Do you remember an encounter with former classmates? The more time that has passed since your last rendezvous, the more easily you recognize their inner and outer changes. Curiously, while all others changed, you remain the same. This illusion also applies in the case of relationship challenges.

Assume you are doing your very best in adapting your actions to make your love and relationship work. But you two seem to speak a different language and live in other worlds. As your efforts for holding the relationship together failed, you conclude that the problem has to be related to your partner. As you are still the same, he is the one who changed. Isn't this a crazy idea? While everything and everyone experiences change as life evolves, you assume that you yourself are the only one excluded from this process? This is a dangerous illusion and may lead to the thought:

He is no longer the person I committed to.

Rather than seeking a path to bring you closer together, you allow this illusion to guide you away from each other. You risk losing your common love. When this mindset appears, your inner alarm immediately has to sound! Open your eyes! Start seeing who you are. You may dislike some aspects of the real picture about yourself. Then take action! During the journey of this book you will discover ways to grow to be the person you want to be, emanating irresistibility and generating the relationship you love. As you are one part of your relationship's bond, your personal growth will have impact. When you step out of your usual routine, your partner is challenged to change, as his old behavior patterns are not working anymore.

The bad ghost of arguing or . . .
The illusion of "Communication is a human gift"

Your man remains resolute in his ways, choosing to ignore the cracks that appear in the relationship? Then "Sorry seems to be the hardest word" may become your relationship's daily song, you sing with Elton John. Maybe during your journey of love he forgot the essence of a woman's heart: it's made to share and be cared about. You hunger for the days when he longed to know your mind and soul, was fascinated to listen and talk. Now he neither shares his feelings nor listens to your challenges and concerns. You see the creeping decay of your communication while the bad ghost of arguing claims more and more space. But communication isn't a human gift!

For many years I shared this illusion with millions of people. Speaking and interacting are interpreted as communication. Even the clear signs of misunderstandings and misconceptions indicating that true communication is not happening become ignored. For your entire life you may act on this illusion and wonder why your love suffers.

Your personal relationship only mirrors the unbridgeable challenges the entire world faces. Communication isn't a human gift! Have you ever played beach paddle ball? This is a wonderful example to illustrate the concepts of daily interaction and true communication. Playing beach paddle you hit the ball to your opposite partner. Unless you are a pro it's a challenge to serve the ball exactly where you want it to go. Your partner does his very best to answer the ball. Sometimes he's lucky, sometimes he fails. If you succeed several times to play the ball continuously back and forth, you assume that communication is established. In fact, communication means to step out of one's world and step into the other's world to see the issue through the eyes of your partner. As the old Indian proverb says:

Don't judge another, until you
walk a mile in their moccasins.

Playing beach paddle ball, you and your partner have each a different sight and perspective of the game. While you may play with the sun towards your back, he plays facing the sun. True communication starts, when one of you two skips over to the other's side. Only when both partners are aligned in the same direction is true communication possible: they speak the "same" language and understand each other's ideas free of misinterpretation. From an early age you learned to put your thoughts into written or spoken words. The focus was always directed only to yourself. You didn't learn to skip over to the other's side to communicate your ideas. The psychological impact of words is not much discussed in education, making coexistences in relationship and love suffer from a lack of understanding. This book dedicates a whole chapter to eliminate this gap of true communication.

The bad ghost transforming your prince into a frog or . . .

The myth of "All men are equal"

Once, a kiss made him your prince. What triggered his transformation back into a frog? Maybe today you wear the entire burden of the shopping bags, because somehow or somewhere he lost the mantle of the Gentleman. And with this loss his compliments, honors and praises are gone. The times may have passed when he recognized your efforts and celebrated your achievements, and enjoyed being at your side and in your life. You may seek the answer to the question . . .

Is this process reversible?
Can the frog be turned back into a prince?

To make this happen you are required to recognize the myth of "All men are equal," as it sabotages your openness and true intention. Regarding the "y" chromosome, men are equal—but that's the only identical pattern. Or would you assume to be the same women as your mother, sister or girlfriend? I know that may sound provocative but it is simply the truth. Nobody is a duplication of someone else. Even monozygotic twins have differences. Maybe they look the same and share common interests but the essence of their being is individual. I agree that men may resonate with some gender-specific behavior. Nevertheless it's essential to step out of the illusion that all men are equal. The reason is obvious! As an example imagine yourself being in a supermarket: why do you choose carefully every fruit that you'd buy? Even if all seem to be the same you know . . . they aren't equal! Acting on this knowledge you fine-tune your perception. You detect the tiny differences between each fruit and act on that information. When you stay connected with the myth that all men are equal you will lose important details of your man. You shift to a superficial picture of him and lose sensitivity for this individuality. Imagine the same thing in reverse. What would be the impact on your relationship's love? Alarming. You are challenged to reawake the fine-tuning of your perception. You will detect the unique "motivation buttons" of your man and will know how to take advantage of them, getting the relationship you want.

The bad ghost transforming you into Cinderella or . . .

The myth of "Love can't be planned"

Once you were his only beloved one, the unique VIP in his life. Your being and personality spread magic in every hour of his day and he was proud to be the one chosen. Once you were his princess, his most precious treasure in life. Those days are gone and today you are only Cinderella, transformed to be his housekeeper. Once you shared your life, now just the house. While romance moved out, a lack of gratefulness moved in. And you think longingly back to the days when he handed roses instead of dirty laundry to you. As love can't be planned, you engage in a journey to resignation.

But that's just another misleading myth making relationship's love vanish. At first glance this misconception seems to make sense. Love grows from the heart, from our feelings, not out of the mind. As falling in love and spontaneity have their roots in the emotional being, cupid's arrow seems to be out of your control. How can a plan be linked with love! Do you remember the spring of your romance, the first months of your falling in love? Don't tell me you didn't plan your rendezvous. Maybe you made yourself pretty, applied a seductive perfume or chose carefully the places of your togetherness . . . you planned your love! When feelings dance the tango, you might be unaware of this fact and ignore it. So, you never transformed this talent of planning into a powerful relationship skill. It remained an impulsive reaction and when stimulations fell asleep you forgot how to take advantage of your special ability. As the minute hand of the clock often dictates the pace of daily life, you may long for a realm of freedom from planning. The sad story is if love is the one without a schedule no time is dedicated to it. Your love is a most important issue. It is worth cultivating your attentiveness. Don't put your relationship behind daily tasks. This book assists you to remodel aspects of your life, giving you a respite to rejuvenate love.

The bad ghost turning happiness into emptiness

Love and relationship should generate happiness in your life. But the years have silenced your laughter; spontaneity and joy have vanished. What happened? Your question forces you to see the emptiness. It also leads you to want to re-awaken happiness in your relationship. You remember being thrown into the waters of love and swimming wonderfully. Now you risk drowning in those waters. While you still are committed to your partner and love, your efforts encounter unknown and mysterious forces. Whatever you do, your efforts vanish in the wind. Challenge the following illusions and myths and banish them out of your relationship's life and word:

Illusion of . . .

"Relationship's reality is touchable"

When a relationship starts shifting to misery your mind looks out for the reasons. That's a natural reaction of the human brain. You need to find an explanation to determine your actions. But this practice shows a crucial misbehaviour, as the human mind equates the individual explanation with the relationship misery. One ignores that the problem may be based on other roots and starts acting on behalf of a limited perception without evidence. So, it's crucial to be aware that the reality of your mind's map isn't the true reality of your relationship. Your mind may be a powerful companion in life when acting on correct principles and truths. But when illusions and myths form the foundation of your decisions, your mind becomes an inner enemy leading you by erroneous ideas to dangerous situations. As a consequence bad thinking may drive you to disrupt your relationship's love. While you act with the best intentions, you destroy your life's happiness by and by. I encourage you to develop a critical mind and enhance yourself as an individual. You will seek a more objective perception of your relationship's reality to get outstanding results. And you clear your mind from the following myth forever:

Myth of . . .

"It's a question of luck: Either a relationship works or not"

"Either a relationship works or it does not." Last week on my way home sitting in the tram I heard that comment accidentally in a conversation between two women. This mindset reflects another illusion limiting woman's power, options and possibilities in their life and love. The words "either" and "or" break the whole in two parts without any link. They are the ones to generate impassable gaps in relationships. In your daily routine you apply the two words either/or countless times. Every action requires a decision. Every decision evaluates options. That's an incorporated process. I must decide to wear either the white or red blouse. Should I call my mother now or later? Most decisions are made on the basis of two options, as this is the easiest way. Unfortunately this method excludes other options, placing their impact and results out of your reach. The same happens to the expression "Either a relationship works or not." Don't accept that your creativity and talents are shackled. Don't allow this mindset to assign you a passive role, becoming a victim of this illusion. Eliminate the idea that happiness and fulfillment in love are just a matter of luck. The next illusion proves the contrary!

Illusion of . . .

"Physics and love live in separate worlds"

In the year 1972 at the "American Association for the Advancement of Science" Edward Lorenz gave a famous speech with the title:

"Predictability: Does the Flap of a Butterfly's Wings in Brazil Set Off a Tornado in Texas?" The Butterfly Effect states that a small change on initial conditions can create completely different results in a later state. For many years, people debated whether this effect is a myth or fact. Following the Millennium Exchange in 2002, the American mathematician Warwick Tucker proved it to be correct. As you can't ignore the law of gravity, the Butterfly Effect is part of your love and relationship. Its physical law is a daily fact and shows its results. Trash the illusion that physics of the Butterfly Effect is an irrelevant factor in love. Take advantage of it! As a little change in your reaction may generate great results you may profit from the leverage.

Did you ever hear about Dr. John Gottman, a professor of psychology at the University of Washington and relationship expert? He has a proven hit rate of 93% regarding his estimate if a relationship is going to survive the next four years. How is this possible? A study conducted by him revealed that the true source of long-term successful relationships is hidden in small and specific daily habits and behaviors.

Consciously changing small habits gives you the key to transform your relationship's world. Being aware of the

Butterfly Effect you have the key to a loving and fulfilled relationship. And finally: You won't be alone in your mission to love!

Myth of . . .

"Love is a lonely game"

Have you ever been on an excursion trip in an unfamiliar area without map or compass? That's quite challenging, as you need to be attentive constantly to prevent getting lost. Maybe you studied a map before starting your journey, but in reality orientation may look different. Perhaps you're on the right track; nevertheless, you feel insecure. In such a case, you make sure by asking another knowledgeable local hiker. As you journey through this book, feelings of insecurity may surface. Do not worry as I shall provide you with tools. Happiness and fulfilment in love do not have to be a lonely game. Trash this myth! Instead imagine being a beginner who plays tennis. It's obvious that having a training partner makes it more fun and enhances your improvement. As you are not the only woman in the world facing challenges in her relationship you get offered a blog to share your questions and insights. Additionally the learning curve rises faster if the beginner plays with a pro from time to time, as this feedback will transmit a clear vision of the personal progress. So, I am at your side whenever you want. Trash all those illusions and myths and act on facts instead. Detox your love and get the relationship you want. True happiness and love are the most precious values in our world and can't be purchased by any money.

But what do you do now that bad ghosts transformed your prince into a frog over the years? When your relationship's love is in serious danger?

Stay with me and you will learn:

How to make this process reversible!

Reviewing the 9 illusions and myths about love and relationship:

#1: Once committed, always committed

#2: Only he changed

#3: Communication is a human gift

#4: All men are equal

#5: Love can't be planned

#6: Relationship's reality is touchable

#7: It's a question of luck: a relationship either works or not

#8: Physics and love live in separate worlds

#9: Love is a lonely game

Chapter 3

The fairytale about the weaker sex

If I'm honest, I have to tell you I still
read fairytales and I like them best of all.

↝ Audrey Hepburn

There's no doubt that fairytales are an important part
of education as they teach the difference between right
and wrong, good and bad. *Snow White, Sleeping Beauty*
and *Cinderella*: who doesn't know those fairytales? They
enchanted us in childhood and filled our hearts, minds
and souls. But analyzing fairytales you will discover
that only the good, assiduous, humble girls get a prince.
Rebellious, self-willed girls with a strong character are
not appreciated and they undergo a re-education of their
personality. William Shakespeare's comedy *The Taming
of the Shrew*, which has been adapted numerous times
for stage, musical theatre, and film, reflects this message.
Perhaps you know the most famous adaptation: Cole Por-
ter's musical *Kiss Me, Kate* and the film version, starring
Elizabeth Taylor and Richard Burton. The film *10 Things I
Hate About You* is also loosely based on Shakespeare's play.

Their message is all the same: strong women with a sense of pride are not welcome in men's and society's world. As a primary imprint, the metaphors are absorbed in woman's subconscious mind and drive her life. The story of only good girls finding their prince becomes the hallmark of a woman's world, whether she wants it to or not. To make your honeymoon last forever, a clean up of all those dusty beliefs is required. Therefore, a transformation of a relationship is only possible from inside out.

Regardless of what fairytales suggest, males are not the only heroes. Women are not the weak gender, even if you heard that over and over again. Real power doesn't emanate from muscles, it unleashes from your mind! Results are determined by actions and actions are directed by the human mind. Think about all the ambitious women having made our world shift: Joan of Arc, Marie Curie, Amelia Mary Earhart, Margaret Thatcher, Sally Ride—just to name some of them. Creativity, intelligence and knowledge are a most effective cocktail. Add some feelings of motivation and determination and you will be unbeatable. It's basic that you recognize your values as woman in your relationship's universe. We aren't the weaker gender, as we are able to endure the pain of childbirth. The wisdom and laws of nature are far beyond those of our civilization. The importance of women for the survival of our species is crucial. Therefore nature adjusted the DNA code to make us dominate humanity. Women are chosen to guide the fortunes of this world. Meanwhile, girls are still brought up to believe that they are the weaker part of humanity even though woman's health actually proves the opposite. For decades women have long outlived men. Our proverbs emphasize the true strength of a woman:

> Behind every successful man is a woman.
>
> ꙮ Source unknown

I don't intend to convert you into a feminist. I just want you to recognize your true nature and to encourage you to assume your natural talent of leadership. You are required to eliminate the harmful effects of fairytales' brainwashing to start the process of your detoxification. This book will guide you safely and keep you on track. During that whole process I'll be at your side offering abundant assistance and insights. You will throw off the shackles of deception and re-awaken your inner potential. As I already emphasized this shift will have impact on all aspects of your life, as you reframe your person, and as a consequence your entire world. You also will regain your natural role of a VIP in your relationship and redesign the future of your life and love. You are the one who can make your dream come true and transform your partner back into a prince. Open your eyes. See your inner power. Listen to your heart and take the lead to align your relationship to happiness and love. Instead of the myth about the weaker sex, always remember:

> Behind every great man is no one.
> The woman is three steps ahead.
>
> ꙮ Bill Cosby

Chapter 4

Butterfly Habits—the secret game changes in a relationship

We are what we repeatedly do. Excellence, then,
is not an act, but a habit.

◇ Aristotle

When your first fall in love, you soar in 7th heaven. Sooner or later reality catches up. The glow disappears. Struggles enter. That's what happens to many relationships. To keep the glow in your partnership, you must steadfastly develop your personal skills. In professional life, the constant nurturing of your talents and abilities is a daily routine. Evolution in technology is challenging your knowledge. To stay up-to-date you learn to adapt new skills and abilities. You turn the page, over and over again. If you behave like a dinosaur in business, the days of your professional career are numbered. How can one assume that the same principle doesn't apply for relationships? Love is an investment. If you don't care about your investment on a regular basis, the likelihood is high that you are going to lose. Many people are not aware that this principle also is valid in their personal relationship. The quality of your contribution determines the quality of your results. Intellectual (IQ) and emotional intelligence (EQ) are important factors to handle challenges in togetherness with class and style. It's essential to modernize and upgrade communication and relationship skills. They are the critical components that allow you to remain in the 7th heaven of love.

Did you know that real transformation of your life and love comes from a mathematic formula? At the International Coach Federation's Annual Conference the noted coach and speaker Julio Olalla[8] gave a rousing speech about the magic formula for everything happening in your life and relationship. The formula is as follows:

Person + Action = Result

If you tend to be unsatisfied with a result, you normally change your action. This behaviour is an automatic impulse and called implementing learning. For some kind of abilities that method is valuable: learning a language, riding a bicycle or driving a car. But there exist other areas in life when changing an action and expecting to initiate and see better results, things don't significantly change. What happens mostly is that you simply ignore the missing piece of the formula. Changing an action is only one possible way to vary the equation. Drastic shifts in results, relationship and life happen when instead of changing the action, the person herself transforms.

Person + Action = Result

When your perception of reality shifts, options for actions show up that were not even thinkable before. That's the magic key to outstanding results in professional and personal life.

Stop reading for a moment and take your time to consciously embody the power of that revelation. This formula is the key to realize any dream or wish you might have. Be it your relationship or another aspect of your life.

As the way you think defines the way you act upon a situation, thoughts are the roots that generate your habits long-term. Thought and habit are inseparably connected. Therefore your habits reveal your inner personality. Your habits make you win or lose and are part of your subconscious mind. That's the reason why this book isn't just about tips and rules, as you wouldn't achieve real changes in your relationship. The true core to fulfilled togetherness is hidden behind a woman's make-up, in her brain. Your ability to step out from your comfortable, limiting habits is the game changer to create a smart relationship.

Most habits consist of unconscious actions and reactions. They represent your personal program. The only decision you are asked to take is as follows:

*Do I accept to be the victim of my programming
or do I want to be the programmer?*

Maybe your actual situation makes you feel like David, facing Goliath, overwhelmed by the challenges. I understand that this evokes emotions of insecurity and anxiety. But remember: David won over Goliath with the help of just some stones. Regarding changes we tend to be convinced that big results may only be achieved by big actions, efforts and sweat. That simple way of thinking isn't really inspiring and attractive. This is my opinion and I suggest you will agree. What this book aspires is to stimulate another form of thinking, the one that always reaches out for a leverage effect. You will start to think and act on a new level of perception. You are going to fine-tune your receptivity and creativity to detect small opportunities that have a big impact on your relationship and life. But how does one come to know, which habits really generate a leverage effect? And this is the crucial point where *Butterfly Habits!* comes into play. This book will help you to save a lot of time to detect the habits, which are really worth the effort to be internalized. In fact you do not have a simple book in your hand but a reliable guide. Due to its assistance you are able to grow your relationship performance exponentially, while you are detecting your main pillars of change.

You ask about the time it takes to integrate a new habit? Studies reveal inconsistent answers to this question. Years ago there was the opinion that it took about 21 days of continuous, ongoing practice to establish a new habit, while newer investigations refer to two months. But time isn't really relevant. What truly counts is the fact that automatism will show up irrevocably and you will enter a flow of ease. The leverage effect of the Butterfly Habits will simplify your life significantly. You will generate outstanding solutions and results when relationship challenges surface.

**Unconscious
Incompetence**

Conscious
Incompetence

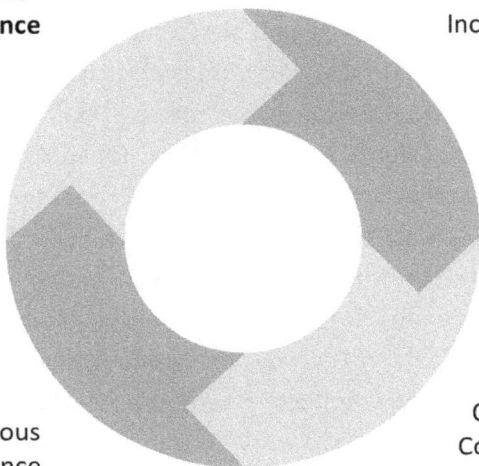

Unconscious
Competence

Conscious
Competence

The moment people start to talk about your luck in love and life you will know that the Butterfly Habits are the true secret of your success.

While you are reading and absorbing these insights your inner transformation follows a natural process: The circle of awareness and growth.[9]

Every change arises from awareness. There is no exception. Therefore awareness is the critical trigger for any improvement in your relationship or life. The problem consists in detecting unconscious inabilities and skills. Referring back to the mathematic formula at the beginning of this chapter: your results are your best indicator. When you feel unsatisfied by them, you know where to look for a solution now. It's not just to select a new action from the options you see right now available, it's more about becoming aware of invisible, unconscious limitations. That's the place where the potential to true leverage resides. Therefore in the moment you gain clarity and awareness about incapacity you also discover a treasure map. You start practicing and establishing the "missing" skill. This phase requires your attention and sensitivity for subtle adjustments. You enter an ongoing process of inner feedback until you have attained the desired results. And one day, while time goes by you will suddenly discover that you automated this specific ability. It became a habit and you don't even need to think about the way and moment to apply it.

The only thing you need to establish selected Butterfly Habits smoothly and gracefully is a smart mind and honest intention. Start your journey and engage your personal transformation of love and life.

Part Two

Butterfly Habits

Chapter 5

One single word makes you shift your
relationship's universe instantaneously

Maybe that's what it all comes down to. Love, not as a
surge of passion, but as a choice to commit to something,
someone, no matter what obstacles or temptations stand
in the way. And maybe making that choice, again and
again, day in and day out, year after year, says more about
love than never having a choice to make at all.

‑‑ Emily Griffin, from *Love the One You're With*[22]

*Something happened. He didn't answer my calls any more.
There was no discussion; nothing that indicated a conflict.
Nevertheless, I instinctively knew that things were off track.
I had a key to his apartment and after my lessons at university I needed to gain clarity about the situation, about us, about
what was happening. I entered the apartment. He was not at
home. And then I saw it, that little envelope on the desk with
my name on it. I instantly recognized his distinctive handwrit-
ing, from the love letters we shared. My heart pounded as I
opened the envelope and started to read:*

You are playing with me and even if I love you deeply,
I can't go ahead with this game.

There it was, black on white; the truth, hidden at the far-
thest angle of my heart. A truth I neither wanted to face nor
to see. In fact, I was a player who wanted to keep all the cards
in her hands. Enjoying our love and relationship, without any
commitment. I sat down on a chair, my head full of thoughts
and at the same time unable to focus on one of them. Here it
was: the moment of a decision that would change everything
from that day on. The world stopped rotating to wait for my
answer. Would it keep turning to the same direction as before,
just going on and leaving all the beautiful experiences and love of
this relationship behind or will my world start to turn towards a
new direction with a common life? I instinctively left all my fears,
friend's comments and prophecies behind and just listened to my
heart. Yes, I loved him and I wanted to have him at my side, as
an important part of my tomorrow's life. I took my lipstick out of
my bag, went to the bathroom and wrote on the mirror:

"I love you"

The one single word

that makes you shift all and everything is called "Commitment." And yes, you are right, it's not the word itself
that changes your relationship. Honestly, it's your unique
energy connected with this word transforming your reality. But what is meant by commitment? Yesterday, I read
an article about being so overcommitted in today's world,

over-committed with doing this and that. But what this person was actually talking about in her article were daily tasks and musts. A commitment is never a must. It is something that comes from the deepest part of your soul; it's connected with a non-negotiable decision, a bond to the goal you are reaching for.

The power of your commitment

is an energy, so strong, that no obstacle is able to stop it. Regardless of the challenges this energy faces, there is a deep and strong connection with faith to overcome all. A solid faith figuring out the way to make your dream come true. Every cell, every atom and molecule of your being is focused on this wish. On one hand, you are pushed towards your goal. On the other hand, you feel a strong attraction by the goal, like from a magnet. There is no place for "musts" or "tasks;" it's just a natural process you and your body, mind, and soul will follow. You know obstacles will show up, from inside and outside, but you also have no doubt that you will overcome them. You strongly believe in the power of this mystical energy inside you. The only thing to do is to trust this energy, listen to its voice and follow the required steps. Maybe you notice a voice of resistance within yourself, to fight everything that shows up to separate you from your aim and dream. A true connection with your commitment triggers a process of sensibility about those processes of resistance—whether they arise from inside or outside. Both are equal in their intention to destroy your commitment. Both try to drive you away from your dream of a wonderful and fulfilling relationship. The strength of your commitment equals the strength of your sensibility regarding those resistances, those patterns, those manipulations.

Ambition is your commitment's best friend

and makes you act on behalf of your dream. Ambition generates endless energy and makes things easier to do. Ambition helps you forget completely about possible obstacles or missing knowledge and practice—it's like a laser light focused on what you want. All other things remain in invisible darkness, out of your mind, out of your perception. And, as perception creates reality, ambition is the most powerful companion on your journey to make your honeymoon last forever.

> Ambition, I have come to believe, is the most
> primal and sacred fundament of our being.
> To feel ambition and to act upon it is to embrace
> the unique calling of our souls.
>
> ᴄᴏ Steven Pressfield, Turning Pro
> and bestselling author of *The War of Art*

The choice of a commitment

respects a basic human need, the need to have options. The difference between "must" and "want" is crucial, as real commitment only arises from your wish. You have the choice to commit for your love in relationship—and you have the choice to let it go. Is there a third option of choice? In connection with commitment there exists just a "yes" or a "no."

I hear you saying: "Ok, Fanny, let's get to the point." Actually I am on the point, the ultimate point that will decide whether there exists a chance to rejuvenate your relationship or not. I firmly believe that your commitment to yourself, to your soul, this solid and untouchable commitment deep inside yourself is the all-deciding force, the fundamental factor for success on this journey. This commitment goes hand in hand with your integrity—your personal decisions about the choice of your thoughts, feelings and behavior.

Your commitment is a secret

a silent promise to yourself. Don't talk about it with anyone. And when I say no one, I really mean it that way. Even your partner, best friend, children, parents are not allowed to know your secret about this commitment. The reasons are obvious. As you are not the only one who is experiencing challenges in relationships, your firm commitment would mirror others' own incongruence, their missing integrity. And—regarding my experiences—they would react upon this like on a provocation. Arguments, stories and discussions will arise to weaken and finally destroy your commitment. As you go your way to a wonderful relationship with your husband, curiosity will arise from outside. In this case just refer people to this book, without further explanation. Your commitment to re-awaken and protect love in your relationship is like your personal treasure map. Your partnership is unique; there is no other relationship as yours. There is no reason for comparison. Your treasure map and your journey are unique. Keep your commitment—to protect love in your marriage—deeply hidden in your heart. It's not something to talk about. Trust me. You are creating a holy place you always can return to in order to recover, to realign, to re-connect with your purpose and dream.

And when time goes by you will realize that this commitment is actually a commitment to yourself, not for your relationship with your partner. It's a commitment to your own happiness in life. It's about the value of your dreams, your person. Just to make it clear, we are not talking about an "ego trip." No, we are talking about reconnection with yourself, regaining focus on what really matters to you. A firm commitment to your happiness and love in relationship will restructure the universe, inside and outside of yourself. It's like a shift of dimension. As you change inside, the world outside of you will transform. Imagine your commitment like water, uniting to a strong river. Everything inside the river flows in one single direction. But also everything outside, getting in touch with the power of water, will align to the same direction, every grass, each leaf, every bush.

The moment of your commitment...

is a holy moment and everybody is aware of this. When a new president agrees to assume responsibility for the whole nation, millions of people watch this moment live on television. People know about the importance of this act. They want to experience the president's commitment that comes from the deepest part of his heart—not his mind. They want to feel the same, what he feels at that very important moment, swearing with his hand on the bible to offer his wisdom and spirit for the best of all the nation's people.

And so it is just natural that a true commitment transforms itself to the highest law to follow. It serves like a light in the darkness of the night. It shows the right way, helps to take the best decision, to readjust importance, to focus the way to the most important dream and wish.

Driving on the island, we spent a wonderful day together. For nearly ten years he was a true friend at my side, sharing the ups and downs of my life. After dinner we went to the terrace to enjoy the sight. The wide fields before us were tinted ochre from the summer's heat. It contrasted with the blue sea at the horizon. Suddenly he took my hand and looked deeply into my eyes, and asked:

Will we be just friends forever, or is there a spark of hope that one day there will be more between us?

You made your commitment a long time ago, before you married. The day of your marriage was just the official demonstration and the sharing of your commitments to the world around you. Like you, and me, each married woman has experienced this special moment. You instantly knew that you had arrived at a point-of-no-return. Time stood still when you decided about the destiny of your relationship. Maybe your heart stopped beating, you stopped breathing in the magic of this moment. Even if you had experienced several of those moments during your journey to love, you knew—at that very instant—that your decision would shift your world.

The risky side of commitment . . .

invaded your thoughts, enhanced your heartbeat when the moment happened. Perhaps you were excited, perhaps you were longing for these unique words, or . . . may be . . . you got surprised by them, like me. With a joke and smile on your lips you could escape answering at that very moment, but the answer was there, waiting. And somehow you started to realize that first of all you had to give the answer to yourself. Maybe you noted a tingling feeling of risk in your body, because guaranteed success in a relationship doesn't exist. Adrenaline and serotonin started to mix up a very explosive cocktail—and you were requested to keep a quiet mind. But hey, the one that threw the question on the table was committed to take that risk. Questions regarding liberty and all common concerns showed up. The more you questioned those thoughts, the more you realized that they were just poor excuses. Your heart won the "showdown" between mind and feelings.

But today the situation has changed. Now, once again you are requested to state a commitment. But this time you know—out of your experience—what the risk is. And in fact there isn't a risk any more. You know, you only can win! And out of this awareness, I encourage you to state your commitment for love and happiness in your relationship. Only by taking small steps you will create results. Therefore take action and join me on ButterflyHabits.com/love-commitment.

On one hand I asked you to keep it secret but on the other hand I know about your wish: you want to share your excitement about this important step with someone. Therefore it would be a gift and honor for me to be that person. You know, at any moment on your journey, I will be at your side to make your honeymoon last forever.

Commitment in the name of love . . .

is the one and unique motivation that unleashes your whole
potential and power within yourself. But what if your mind
tells you over and over again that your partner needs to
change, not you, that you did everything from your side to
make this relationship work? We both know the answer. You
have this book right now in your hands, because you want
to make your honeymoon last forever. You didn't spend your
money for this book if you weren't really open and prepared
to change the course of your relationship to happiness and
love. Maybe you do not feel very confident at the moment,
but listen to me, there will be nothing that you can't master—I promise. To unleash the Butterfly Habit of commitment, it is important to be aware of three different sources of
motivation.[10]

Commitment in the name of love;
Commitment in the name of fear;
Commitment in the name of society.

The one I want you to reach for is the commitment in
the name of love. The motivation of this commitment will
unleash and focus your entire being on the love in your relationship, reconnect you with that special and unique bond to
your partner. On the other hand, all kinds of fears may hide
behind a motivation to commitment. And it is crucial to be
aware of them: fears about losing material things, financial
security and friends. I ask you—just for a moment—to feel
what that kind of fear generates in your body. You start being
aware how your body energy changes. Your breath feels

restricted and perhaps you start noticing a heavy load on your shoulders. Fear as a motivation for a commitment will not generate empowering energy. And it's a simple fact: solid and true love can't arise out of fear. It's just impossible! Fear as the relevant motivation for a commitment is a weak and useless starting point to a loving partnership.

There exists also the possibility of a commitment in the name of society. In this case the voice of society talks to you in your mind. What you "must" do, to be part of a community, of a family. Religious belief may keep you tied. If those are the hidden motivations of your commitment, then you are cheating yourself about love. You are just trying to keep the image of a good relationship alive, as a facade for others. You will miss the power of your heart to persistently follow your goal. Real commitment is only and exclusively about the love between you and your partner— and love arises only from love.

I invite your right now, while you are still connected with those insights, to discover your personal motivation patterns. Ask yourself:

*What spirits drive **my** commitment?*

Please remind yourself: This is not a test, like at school. There exists no right or wrong answer. It's just about you: what you feel and think at this very moment in your life and in your relationship. It's about evaluating your personal "here and now." Knowing, where you start from will offer a huge help to evaluate the specific assistance you need, to identify which alignments have to be focused on finally connect you with the ultimate commitment power within yourself. I am at your side to ensure that you go ahead step by little step, integrating the power of each little shift and insight into a Butterfly Habit. Today we tend to think rushing is the only way to move somewhere—but as I emphasized in the introduction of this book—most people ignore the power of Butterfly Habits. A tiny shift might cause a huge turn-around. What you will learn in this book is to make tiny shifts at the crucial points. Studies[11] show that one of the crucial factors causing relationships to fail is a lack of commitment. And that's the reason why I want you to start right now at this point. Making a commitment is always something like a jump into the unknown. The questions are:

Am I making this jump or not?
Do I commit to protect my relationship's love
like a mother protecting her child?
Am I determined to fight for love?

A commitment changes the rules of your world . . .

and as a consequence something that was important before, may be unimportant now. Something different suddenly gets top priority in your life. A shift of priority creates a shift in your whole life. It is not astonishing when insecurity and anxiety show up, when a commitment has to be stated. You are asked to enter a new world with new challenges and you don't even know what kind of challenges these will be. But you profoundly believe in yourself. You know that you are doing the right thing and finally you deeply trust your inner voice, no matter what will show up. And here you are again: aligned with your personal integrity, bound to your commitment.

What we are talking about here is related to your potential, your personal growth. This kind of commitment is light-years away from conceding. It is a deep connection with yourself, your wishes, your dreams, the love you deserve to experience in your relationship.

Commitment makes you fly . . .

if it grows out of the right motivation. And there is another factor and that's what you feel about your commitment. How strong is the energy behind your commitment?

I ask you to rank the strength of your commitment, on a scale from one to ten.

You strengthen your personal position by knowing the grade of your commitment, as another ultimate indicator to support you in making your honeymoon last forever. Rating from one to ten, I would like to have your commitment on ten. I want you to know and feel that you will recover a fabulous relationship with your partner. Nothing and no one, not even misleading behavior patterns of your loved one, will stop you from achieving this goal. This book develops its power, if you are fully committed. Therefore I would like to encourage you to take advantage of Three Butterfly Habits to Strengthen Your Commitment on ButterflyHabits.com/commitment-strength. Let go of insecurity. Ignore your inner voice telling yourself stupid things like "I can't." It's just not true! How many times in your life have you already proven the unbeatable power of your commitment? I am deeply convinced that the power of commitment is part of your being.

Maybe, you are just not fully aware of it. When commitment comes to action, it's mostly a subconscious process. It's not that you tell yourself, "I commit to this and nothing will get me away from it." In your many daily thoughts there—just for a second—is a tiny thought that made magic happen. Perhaps you didn't notice this thought or forgot about it. What you never will forget are the results that arose out of it. If extraordinary results show up, most people start to talk about luck. But it was never a question of luck. It was a logical process, an unstoppable result of your commitment. That tiny little decision in your brain, even if you forgot about it.

Commitment makes you drive the car . . .

because you stop complaining about all the things you don't like to happen. You start focusing on these two questions:

"What did I commit for?
What do I want?"

This is going to change the universe around you, because you step into the power of responsibility. You liberate yourself from weakness and complaints and start to be creative. You connect with the genius within yourself, finding extraordinary solutions for every situation and challenge. And you connect with a genius that doesn't act on behalf of an ego, but looks instead for win-win solutions.

Reintegrating consciously the Butterfly Habit and power of commitment in your daily being is one of the most important steps in this book, your journey to a fulfilled relationship. Training your awareness about commitment shifts your life.

A world of possibilities opens...

its gate, when you commit entirely. Do you know the "9-dot-mystery?" This game demonstrates the effect of a commitment in a brilliant and simple way. The challenge consists in connecting all 9 dots by four straight lines, without ever lifting the pen. Below I encourage you to play and find the solution yourself:

Find the solutions of the 9-dots-mystery at ButterflyHabits.com/dots.

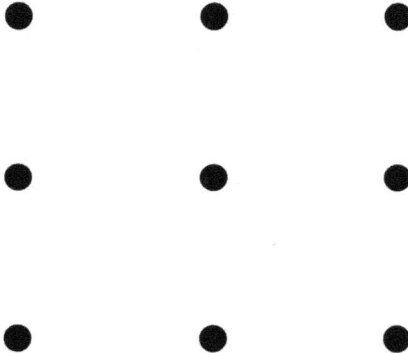

What shows up is that the solution lies outside the 9-dots area. It requires thinking outside the box.

In a daily routine you tend to search solutions for challenges inside the 9-dots frame. Either your options are very limited or there doesn't exist a solution—as the 9-dots game illustrates. You feel destructive emotions of frustration and incapacity. Being connected with your commitment generates a shift in dimension. You start to look for solutions outside of the normal frame, the normal behavior. Your genius awakes and invisible options become visible to you. That's the Butterfly Habit and power of commitment. It opens a gate to get outside of your comfort zone. Commitment is the force that helps you to overcome fears, face obstacles and ignore your "ordinary" habits. It's the source that makes people succeed.

You reach out for a goal that is worth fighting for and your commitment is the energy that makes this dream come true. The journey to "make your honeymoon last forever" is like climbing a mountain. And I am sure you already have some experience on that. You know it's not a question of speed to reach the summit. First of all it's a question of commitment. If you are not fully committed to climb the mountain, you will give up when first obstacles arise. You know that you have to define intermediate goals that— one by one—direct you closer to the top of the mountain. Those "little" goals provide you a rest, to regain energy, to celebrate and honor the attainments and . . . to reconnect with your commitment. Without commitment the summit of the mountain never will be attained.

But keep aware of the difference between true

commitment and task. True commitment awakens the energy and power that motivate you to keep going ahead. It generates a non-negotiable will, energizing every cell of your being. Claim your right to live a loving marriage and commit to your happiness!

Reconnecting with the title of this chapter, I have to confess that I cheated. It isn't one single word that makes shift your relationship's universe—in fact there are two words:

I commit

Butterfly Habit of Commitment

Every morning before starting your day and every night before going to sleep practice the following exercise to sharpen your sense of commitment:

Get a little mirror, just big enough to see your eyes.

Take a deep look into your eyes and say the following commitment to yourself in a loud, determined voice: I commit to protect my relationship's love, to handle any challenge with style and class.

Repeat it, until you feel the power of commitment in your entire being.

Chapter 6

Four Butterfly Principles for avoiding incongruence and making you love who you are

Who in the world am I? Ah, that's the puzzle.

∽ Lewis Carroll, *Alice in Wonderland*

"The magic happens after two weeks," the old man said and he pushed anther olive in his mouth. "You can see it in the eyes: the mask falls. You see the true being of the person. This moment is as beautiful as the individual you have the honor to get to know."

I was only a week on the pilgrim way to Santiago de Compostela in Spain, wondering if this would also happen to me. I followed an inner voice that told me to go on this adventure two weeks ago. I went to a trekking shop, bought the equipment and started at Jaca, a little village in the Spanish mountains. The energy of the mystic ancient pilgrim's way enchanted instantly. Early in the morning I started to walk without knowing where I was going or where I would sleep at night.

*No plans, no maps, just following the yellow painted arrows
on walls, streets, stones. Six hours, day by day. My sensual
awareness increased while my mind slowed down. I noticed
every single ant crossing my way and . . . then it happened. I
still remember the smell of the earth, the sun's heat on my
skin and the intense blue of the lake in front of me. Suddenly
I knew what was important for me, what was useless in my
life's backpack, how much less I needed to feel deeply happy
and fulfilled. The first time in life I saw my face in the mirror,
without the mask.*

This chapter is not about you having to change, because
you are all right the way you are. You are here with me,
because you did what you did, experienced what you experienced and are the person you are. Change is the only secure
thing in this world. Yesterday you were another person than
you are today and will be tomorrow. It's not astonishing that
you may forget who you were on your life's pilgrimage. The
biggest revelation is when you discover that you don't even
know who you are in this present moment. How can you
even believe to know who your partner is? Your relationship
is a pilgrim's journey throughout life. The more self-awareness, self-esteem, self-confidence and self-security you gain,
the more yellow arrows will show up to guide you to your
relationship's fulfillment. Those four "S-Words" charac-
terize the basic principles to "Make Your Honeymoon Last
Forever."

Butterfly Principle #1

Authenticity serves you; wise authenticity serves your relationship.

The package you sold to your partner, is it still valid? Do you remain the person you were, when he fell in love with you? I know, this question may sound like a provocation. But thinking about those two questions assists you to re-connect with your inner core. The problem is that you not only tend to forget who you were, you also tend to forget about important individual facets and values of your being. Deep inside you may feel lacking and incomplete. Remembering the person you were shifts your awareness on what you are missing in today's life. Integrating and revitalizing these parts in your present person generates authenticity. If you are authentic, you are connected with your true being. Authenticity empowers, inspires and requires wisdom. An authentic reaction generates constructive results, when it's based on the savvy part of your personality. The authenticity I am talking about is a "wise authenticity." It is a conscious choice in contrast to an impulsive reaction and it creates options, grows love and trust in your relationship.

If you have the opportunity then join me on Butterfly-Habits.com/authenticity. Let's dive in a little bit deeper to reveal your personal, wise authenticity.

Butterfly Principle #2

Integrity arises when you keep the promises to yourself, not only to others.

The "Applause-Syndrome" is the most underestimated factor in personal growth from being a child to adulthood. A baby needs the parents' love. The child seeks the recognition of his peers at school, a pay raise at work confirms for adults that they are appreciated. The personal self-esteem is mainly calibrated to external indicators and is thus at the mercy of others. Right now I challenge you to honor yourself; to be proud of your achievements, to recognize your courage, to appreciate your growth despite some errors. You are an amazing and gorgeous being. A unique miracle of evolution. Nothing and no one is in a position to prove the contrary! There is no need to impress others. The only person in this universe, who is worthy of impressing is you. Without integrity you live the life of a zombie. How can you expect that you would nourish your relationship's love if you lack integrity? It's simply impossible! Keep firm to the promises you made to yourself because you are important and crucial to the fate of your life and relationship.

Challenges to strengthen your integrity

- Declare your decision to act with integrity and keep promises to yourself. Because every small action creates the life and relationship you want!

Ask yourself:
- Which promise to myself didn't I keep?
- Would this promise still support my relationship dream?

- In case of yes: what would be the next step to keep this promise?
- Position yourself each morning and evening before a mirror and look deep into your eyes. Say in a loud voice to yourself: I am important. I keep my promises to myself.
- Practice this exercise until you have a clear "Yes!" in how you feel.
- When facing challenges in your relationship always ask yourself: If I were essential in our partnership, what would I do for it?

Butterfly Principle #3

Congruency is the highway to your dreams.

What's more important in life than knowing who to be and where to go? After continuing your journey to wise authenticity with the assistance of my website discovery-tool, you gained much more clarity about who you are. The next step is to know where to go. Why is this so meaningful? When you know where to go, what your dreams and wishes are, you nourish your self-security. Self-security is an inner state of being, empowering you to maintain balance in challenging moments of life. Self-security is like a lighthouse in the dark night of your fears and doubts. You can't get lost, because its light unleashes your internal power and determination. Self-security generates congruency to your inner world and to your decisions and behavior. Knowing your dreams and knowing the target awakens your sleeping potential.

But mostly dreams and goals are made regarding the expectations of others. If those are out of the norm, they are dismissed as fantasies. We want an extraordinary life, but we lack the courage and confidence to reach for the stars. As long as you define dreams from the outside, you won't attain happiness and fulfillment inside. You will lack self-security and congruency, because deep inside you can't cheat yourself. You can't lie to your own heart when it comes to dreams and wishes. Your mind may try to convince you from a logical point of view. But self-security and congruency only can awaken and grow from a goal that is truly yours. Congruency means following the inner call to make your dreams come true. Let's consider how to gain self-security, how to build congruency in thoughts, feelings, decisions and behavior.

Like re-connecting with your wise authenticity and integrity, congruency is a journey from inside out requiring some patience and dedication.

And one thing is certain: congruency is already part of your personality, abilities and being—you just need to strengthen it.

> You cannot teach a man anything;
> you can only help him find it within himself.
>
> ～ Galileo Galilei

Every muscle of your body needs to be trained, or it loses power and strength. Maybe you are jogging, dancing, practicing yoga. Whatever you do, you are consciously working on the health of your muscles. The same happens to your mind. Imagine reading the same newspaper every day.

What will happen? The synapses of your brain will degenerate. Just as a record, you'll end up only having a single deep groove. The ability of your mind will be reduced to a "micro-world" with poor flexibility.

In addition to body and mind exist other muscles that urgently need to be trained; muscles that have a huge impact in our life. I am talking about the muscles of our emotions. In school we are not taught how to use these specific muscles. Imagine the power of courage, the power of will, the power of love, the power of passion. They all are part of your being but you never learned how to activate them individually in challenging situations. Self-security and congruency are strongly bonded to your emotions. Training the muscles of your emotional world, you get access to the most powerful source inside you. When you are driven by an emotion of passion, nothing and no one can stop you. Knowing how to push those muscles' "start" buttons you create an immense shift inside and outside yourself. Changing your emotion from fear to courage opens you to a world of new options and possibilities. These specific emotions are the secret, where true self-security and congruency awaken.

Empowering muscle training

Choose a challenge or remember a past experience and generate a specific emotion.

- Try to increase the feeling to a top intensity of 10 (note the value you attain).
- When the emotion reaches its highest intensity, press softly the point at your body where you feel it.

- Finally, look in a big mirror and observe the changes in facial expression and body posture (note them for another chapter's exercise).
- Every time you want access to that specific emotion press softly the referring point of your body and reconnect with the state.

Empowering Muscle Group	Intensity (Rating 1 to 10)	Where in the Body?	Changes of Facial Expression & Body Posture?
Gratitude			
Courage			
Will			
Love			
Passion			

As you know it takes about two months to establish a new habit. But what are two months in comparison to a lifelong profit from this exercise? Nothing, believe me. It cannot be stressed enough that the question of time shouldn't have relevance. In the same way as you decide to learn a foreign language, to dance, paint or ski the decision for integration of a new habit shouldn't depend on whether it takes a week, a month or a year. Therefore, I recommend activating some personal tactics to stay on track with the training of your "Power-Emotions." Set different alarms on your phone, block time in your personal agenda, place visual memo stickers in your home and/or at work. And most important of all to successfully strengthen the emotions of your personal congruency: Remember your amygdala and do tiny, effortless training sessions—on a daily base!

Besides your inner dreams and power-emotions, there exists another factor to enhance your self-security and congruency. This factor resides in the principle of "A Woman's pillars." For women it is crucial to build their life's "roof" not on one single pillar.[12] If this pillar gets damaged the whole life's "roof" is in danger. The more pillars exist, the more self-security increases. Based on the fact of gender-specific differences in the brain, studies show that women tend to be relationship-oriented in their thinking. If a woman's relationship is the only pillar of her life's roof she tends to overreact. Even the smallest disparities trigger her inner light "red alert." A secure way out of this dilemma is to create and build further pillars; pillars that enhance a woman's independence.

This is not about distancing yourself from your partner, it is about taking responsibility for your emotional balance. Your partner will profit from it. What kind of pillars could these be? A new job, a voluntary engagement, going back to school, whatever supports your feeling of independence. The biggest enemy of a fulfilled relationship is convenience.

Stepping out of your comfort zone and creating new pillars for your life's roof is a doable challenge. Just remember your inner dreams and wishes. They are essential to unleashing powerful motivation and determination. I encourage you to become an architect of your life's roof and build additional pillars to integrate self-security and congruency forever. Keep the Butterfly Effect in mind: by taking one small step at a time, even when it seems insignificant, your self-security will grow and nourish your emotional balance.

Create your "woman's life roof"

Find a quiet place, lean back, close your eyes and let your mind flow about the following questions:

- In a rating from 1 to 10 (10 = maximum), what is my feeling of independence in my relationship?
- What is my actual life's roof situation? How many pillars exist?
- Which are 10 further pillars for my life's roof? (Note them without judging)
- What specific pillar would most strongly support my self-security and congruency?
- What would be the next little step to start creating this pillar?

Butterfly Principle #4

Trust builds bridges to your dreams, from nothing.

How do you react when obstacles and challenges arise on the way towards a goal? Is it ignoring, courage, self-confidence, or trust that makes you go ahead? All of those factors are powerful. Ignoring is an effective method when your inner voice starts its manipulation game with fears and doubts. As long as you don't ignore valid information that requires a realignment of your path towards the stated goal, your journey will be secure. Ignoring stands on its own, while self-confidence aligns with courage and trust. Self-confidence nourishes your courage to reach out to the seemingly impossible. Courage draws you to act from your inner lion's heart. Heroines are born out of this lion's heart quality.

You also can demonstrate a kind of courage right now.

You prove yourself a brave heart when you make your honeymoon last forever. Now consider self-confidence: a significant subtle energy. Self-confidence and trust strengthen each other. Even in the darkest night when all seems lost, as a heroine you follow your calling. Trust your inner wisdom. Be confident and keep on following your inner voice. Trust that somewhere, somehow, a door will open and a solution will appear. It is like sailing in the darkness of the sea towards your harbor. You know that the lighthouse will appear from nowhere and lead you safely home. It is trust that nourishes your self-confidence and courage to reach out for the stars of your life and relationship. Trust is a feeling to be exercised. Trust is a verb. Act on it!

Chapter 7

The true enemy of your relationship's happiness hides inside your mind

The soul is placed in the body like a rough diamond,
and must be polished, or the luster of it
will never appear.

⌐ Daniel Defoe, author

*The blood rushed through my veins, as did my thoughts
through my mind. For the first time in our partnership, I was
furious and anxious at the same time. How would he react? I
was right and he was wrong, sure. But to lose my inner balance of power made me feel weak and dependent. I never experienced jealousy before, this horrible feeling of insecurity and
suspicion. The words in my mind tormented me. I had to stop
this inner voice immediately! I came off my chair and ran out
of the house. I ran up the hill to the nearby forest. My heart
raced. My breathing tried to adjust to my physical exertion.
Minute by minute, I felt better. I regained the power over my
mind; the destructive spirit of my inner voice gone.*

According to Deepak Chopra, you have about 65,000 thoughts per day! You process information from outside as well from inside yourself. To keep from being overwhelmed, your mind has to filter them, to delete parts of the information. Unfortunately this process can also cut off valid information, creating an illusion of reality. Therefore your personal reality isn't equal to the "real" reality. Your partner, as well, is bound to this natural process and he perceives his own "reality." That's the way different perceptions of a situation arise and affect discussions or generate arguments in partnership. The only way to escape this pattern are the following Butterfly Habits:

Mind-Shift #1

Mistrust your mind

Be aware of the fact that you and your partner see the world through different eyes. Neither of you two knows the reality that the other sees and that triggers the sparkle of healthy mistrust. While mistrust generally focuses on the other person, this kind of mistrust focuses on the perception of your own mind. That's the seed for huge achievements in the human world. That's the way a scientist approaches reality. Curiosity is a wonderful catalyst to assist you in this mind-shift and to establish this new habit. Curiosity makes you step out of your own tight borders while you watch out for the unknown. Discussions with your partner cease to be about who is right or wrong. Instead you will start digging for the differences in the perception of a situation, collecting valuable information. That's the spirit guiding you to inner growth and understanding of your and your partner's world. Knowing to question your own perception is your starting point to excellence in the "inner game." It rejuvenates your mind and . . . a young mind is sexy!

Mind-Shift #2
Make each day a "Groundhog Day"

Have you seen the film "Groundhog Day" with Bill Murray and Andie McDowell? It's simply a must! Bill Murray, playing the role of a weatherman, is caught in a time loop, living the same day over and over again. After a while, the weatherman begins to make the best of his day. He had nothing to lose, since he began every day anew. This shift in his mindset initiated his personal transformation as well as a change of his world.

I am a big fan of this wonderful metaphor, demonstrating the huge effect of a tiny change in thoughts.

Take a minute and meditate about the following questions:

> *When each day offers you a new opportunity:*
> *How would your perception about failure change?*
> *What would you risk right now to improve happiness*
> *in your relationship?*

The concept of failure would get replaced entirely by the concept of growth. Each day you would just observe the results and let the past go. Perhaps you may struggle with a challenge, but you never fail. Each attempt would bring you closer to the goal: like a child learning to walk, step by step without self-criticism. This would be your greatest win from this Butterfly Habit. You would approach each day like a painter approaches a blank canvas: full of curiosity. A mind-shift in the concept of failure unleashes the power for amazing changes in your relationship. Let the past go, just keep your lessons!

Mind-Shift #3

Expectations are the ticket to dependence

Nobody likes to be dependent. Nevertheless, we develop unconscious habits that drive us into dependence on others. The crazy thing is that we cling to habits, even if those habits show miserable results. Having expectations is exactly one of those habits.

At the beginning of this book I emphasized the power of the "Butterfly-Effect." The name of the effect was coined by Edward Lorenz, a pioneer in the chaos theory. His famous speech entitled "Predictability: Does the Flap of a Butterfly's Wings in Brazil Set Off a Tornado in Texas?" shifted our world's mindset drastically.[1] The Butterfly Effect states that in non-linear systems predictability becomes impossible. But in daily life saying or doing something out of an expectation, you predict the result. You forget that expectations are subject to the Butterfly Effect. The possibility of achieving exactly the expected result you wish is like playing roulette. It's minimal, as the illustration demonstrates. Usually by doing or saying something you expect one specific reaction—indicated by the black arrow. But the nature of the Butterfly Effect actually generates many different possibilities of reactions you don't consider. Referring to the graph below there is a total of 18 options, not only a single one. Therefore the chance of being disappointed is very high.

The Probability that an Expectation is Fulfilled

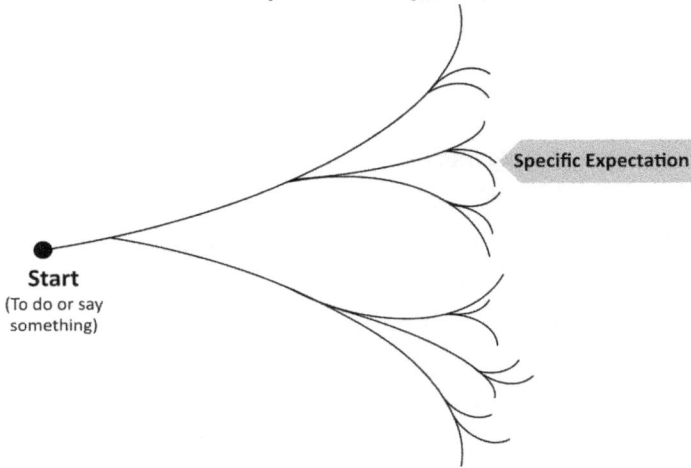

Specific Expectation

Start
(To do or say
something)

To ensure long-term success in love, delete expectations from your mind. Being free of expectations strengthens your emotional balance, the perception of reality and your relationship's harmony.

Problems in relationships arise, when expectations don't get fulfilled!

Make it a Butterfly habit to ask yourself always:

In saying or doing this, what do I expect of my partner?

Mind-Shift #4

Offsetting is the slide into dependence

This kind of thinking is one of the most destructive habits for a relationship. Stop doing it immediately. It arises from your enemy's voice inside of your head, stirring anger. It contaminates your body, mind and soul. If you become aware of the habit to offset or counter balance, set limits rigorously to this nagging inner voice.

"If he would do this, then I would do that" is a kind of thinking that ruins relationships. Offsetting is just doing things from the perspective of an expectation. And once again you fall for this mindset. Who is the judge to define the value of one action versus another action? What is easy to do for one person can be difficult to do for another. Injustices are inevitable. Your motivation for doing something should consist in a positive purpose, independent of others! On one side you have this tormenting inner voice, but on the other side your mind is a genius. Each moment you can create various ideas and inspirations to motivate yourself. I am not talking about making your partner a pasha! I just want to emphasize that the Butterfly Habit of knowing your personal motivation buttons allows you to take control of happiness and success in your life and relationship.

Mind-Shift #5
There's neither a frog, nor a prince

Nature has provided specific roles for males and females to ensure survival. While evolution increased our mental capacities, our reptile brain still has that original programming stored. In a subconscious way it keeps influencing you. On one hand, women of today's generation enjoy a freedom our grandmothers could only dream of. And because of this we keep seeking equality in our male dominated world. On the other hand, there is this little reptile in our brain, whispering to search for the special one in our life, to create a family. No wonder that women as well as men get confused. The sword of Damocles hangs over our relationships with the threat to leading to divorce. Fairytales and teenagers' movies still reflect the old spirit of male and female role in society; creating unrealistic expectations. As a frog never can become a human, a man never will mirror the perfect prince. The perfect prince is able to anticipate your dreams and wishes. He has a direct link to your thoughts and emotions. He is inside your skin! Woman's expectation is based on a myth that makes a man crazy. He isn't perceived just as a human being, with strengths and weaknesses. Set your expectations apart and start to face reality. Take note of both of your given talents and make it a habit to offset one's weaknesses by the other's strengths. This is the secret of great and powerful partnerships.

Mind-Shift #6

Make your relationship's rules dinosaur free

Trash the society rules! Start creating your own rules! Like a coin, rules have two faces. On one side they bring clarity in your relationship; simplifying the common life, creating the pillars of your love. Relying on that side, you feel secure. Relationship rules are an intimate issue, growing from the depths of your hearts. They are your silent promise to act on behalf of each other. Creating your personal relationship rules is the best way to protect your love as well as keeping both of your individualities, as they are bonded to your daily habits. Also, rules set borders that you are going to define yourselves. For one couple narrow borders work well, while others need more leeway. There's no right and wrong as long as both partners commit fully to the stated rules and act on behalf of them.

On the other side, there exist countless little, never negotiated rules in relationships. Here they are in your life, a wanted or unwanted influence of your behavior. Think about the Butterfly Effect and begin to question the usefulness of such rules. Are there some dinosaurs? How could such rules be upgraded, enhancing both of your lives' quality and habits?

Checking rules is an ongoing process and secures your long-term success in love. Care about your rules and design a relationship life style you both enjoy.

Get some insights about your relationship's rules.

What's the procedure in your relationship to define rules?
How do you ensure that both partners stay aware of these rules?
Which rules are static and which ones are negotiable?
What kind of habits and behavior will they generate?
How do you ensure that partnership rules
don't become dinosaurs?

Mind-Shift #7

90% of all fears are an illusion

Fear can be as big as an elephant or as little as a flea. Fear can make you flee in full panic or be bound by a subtle insecurity. The former you are aware of, while the latter you hardly realize. Studies have proven that people become motivated more effectually by fear than by dreams. And our society takes full advantage of this knowledge. Fear is an ever-present part of our lives and is one of the best-proven instruments of manipulation. Not just you but also your relationship is exposed to this influence. Fear is one of the biggest challenges we face in life. Susan Jeffer's book Feel the Fear and Do it Anyway® is a great additional resource, in case you and your life are contaminated by this destructive emotion. To fight against fear requires courage, will and determination. It requires a precious goal like . . . love. If you are able to face your fears, you are able to face anything in life. The enemy inside our mind called fear is just an illusion. Studies indicate that 90% of our fears never become reality.[13] Imagine the unnecessary weight on your shoulders that you carry in your lifetime.

90% of your fears can be thrown overboard immediately!
How would that change your life in light of this perspective?

Get rid of unnecessary fears

In your diary, create a list with all "big" and "little" fears. Take several days to complete this list, as many fears will surface, one by one, from your subconscious mind. Then write behind each fear the sentence "90% of this is rubbish!"

Take your time to feel the emotional release of your body and soul.

Maybe some fears will become irrelevant, while some others will refuse to go away. Whatever will be the result, I encourage you to stick with this mind training and make it a daily habit. Sooner or later results will turn up, trust me.

The only way to get rid of a persistent fear is to face it. It will poison your being as long as you don't confront it.

When your decision to liberate yourself from this bad ghost isn't negotiable any more, your determination will conquer your fear. You can learn to be a heroine! Remember the last chapter when I wrote about empowering muscle training? To train your muscle of courage should become a Butterfly Habit. When you feel somehow, somewhere, inner resistance based on insecurity or fear, face it! I don't encourage you to put your life in danger. I just want you to act like in the fitness centre. You start with a little challenge and increase it from day to day. That's your secure journey to become your life's and relationship's heroine. For further assistance get the mini-guide 10 Empowering Butterfly Habits to Face Fears & Doubts on ButterflyHabits.com/mini-guide.

A review of "the enemy in your mind":

Mind-Shift #1: Mistrust your mind
Mind-Shift #2: Make each day a "Groundhog Day"
Mind-Shift #3: Expectations are the ticket to dependence
Mind-Shift #4: Offsetting is the slide into dependence
Mind-Shift #5: There's neither a frog, nor a prince
Mind-Shift #6: Make your relationship's rules dinosaur free
Mind-Shift #7: 90% of all fears are an illusion

Chapter 8

Taking the lead in the name of love shifts your relationship's destiny

I am not afraid . . . I was born to do this.

⤳ Joan of Arc

"Cast off!" Starting for a sailing trip, everything happens easy and gracefully: We agree about the target destination, set a navigation course regarding wind and weather conditions and trim the sails. On board, the Captain holds the responsibility that crew and boat arrive safe and sound at the destination. I still remember the little, bronze plate on the bunkwall of our sailing boat:

RULE #1: The Captain is always right.

RULE #2: If the Captain is wrong, see Rule #1.

Usually a Captain involves his crew in the decisions to be taken. Nevertheless, in case of an emergency, there is no time for discussion. Instead, fast action is requested to avoid the worst-case scenario. That's the moment when the Captain takes responsibility for the good of all.

On board, we harmonized. We were a wonderful sailing team. But in our relationship, it was a different story. I often got the feeling while sitting together in the boat that we had no navigation course, no target destination, no sails set. Both of us were unhappy, felt misunderstood—neither of us really taking responsibility. Finally I discovered the obvious:

A relationship needs a Captain!

I want you to make yourself the Captain of your relationship. I encourage you to take the lead—in the name of love. Don't wait until your "relationship-boat" runs aground and sinks. As long as your relationship's boat is still floating, there is time to change its course. To take the lead doesn't mean to hang the Captain's rules on the wall. This would only provoke discussion and there is no time for discussion. It's time to take action. To take the lead is a personal, inner decision, similar to your commitment. While the commitment was a promise by you and to you, taking the lead means assuming the responsibility for the good of both. You take the rudder in your hand to get your relationship on the "right" course. You may say, "Why me, not him?" Taking the lead connects you with your inner power. You step out of the victim's role to learn and grow. You stop blaming your partner, looking for a patsy. On the contrary, as you progress through this book's journey, you will inspire your partner.

There is no need to talk about this new habit of taking the lead. Subconsciously your partner will be aware that something has shifted and that you are behaving differently. Your decision to lead in the name of love, to make a difference in your relationship, initiates the "Butterfly-Effect," and may generate a drastic turn-around in your relationship's world.

Taking the lead inspires...

your creativity. As the responsible Captain of your relationship's boat, you are looking for options, solutions. You can't afford to complain about a problem, while the boat still holds its course toward a reef. By living your relationship out of this role, you automatically shift your perception, your thinking and your behavior. Even your feelings change from helplessness and frustration to determination. Maybe you don't like your present relationship's situation, but as a Captain you are more interested in getting the course corrected in the right direction: toward your target. This focus activates your whole, inner potential. You get sensitized to options and possibilities. And even facing a big challenge, you feel more comfortable, because you know you are the captain and you have all cards in your hand. Additionally, you act as a model, an inspiration to your partner. You animate him to grow and learn, as well as to remember the common dream of your intimate bond. Some years ago in a seminar, Deepak Chopra spoke about happiness in life. Scientific studies reveal the impact of other people's energy on our personal energy. As an example, Chopra remarked that sharing time with a happy person leverages your own happiness about 15%. When taking the lead in the name of love, your determination, your optimism, your behavior inspires your partner. Your energy penetrates subconsciously all levels of his being. When you take the lead, your relationship can't resist changing.

Leadership with class and style . . .

is requested when adapting this role in your partnership. It's not about being the boss from today on and giving orders and instructions to your partner. In being a leader, you are asked to reveal your inner light, to serve intentionally as a model. Don't take every single word or reaction as a confrontation or even as a failure. Failure doesn't exist, just results, learning and growing. Leaders are not born; leaders are made by their experiences. Every challenge embraces a countless amount of potential to become better. Your partner's reaction is your feedback on your behavior as a leader. I encourage you to approach this role like a game. Be humble with yourself—you are just beginning to be a leader. Honor each of your little steps, even each of your efforts, regardless of the results. Doing and trying is the golden way to great leadership. And the final gain of a wonderful relationship is worth the effort and sweat, trust me. Taking the lead is like starting a journey full of adventures. You never know what will happen. Excitement as well as surprises will become part of your personal growth. And the further you proceed, the more you win security and trust in your own potential and enjoy your leading role in the name of love.

Entrepreneurial spirit in love . . .

helps you to stay focused on the big goal. As the entrepreneur in your relationship, you flow in a river of awareness. You constantly train your abilities; you initiate the necessary adjustments and corrections if you notice that you are off course. You adapt a high flexibility on changing environments and situations. You learn from the past and integrate your enhanced wisdom in the present. The only time that counts for you is this moment. It's just here and now where you hold all options in your hand. As an entrepreneur of your relationship's love, you leave the past behind and do right now the very best to approach tomorrow's goal. Do you notice how your energy changes, while reading these words? You are starting a new life style! By integrating an entrepreneurial approach, your whole being shifts. When you start to think BIG, you can't afford to waste your energy in resentments. When others resign, you keep on going, regardless of the obstacles. You believe in your dream and trust in an inner, higher guidance. You ignore the whispering inner voice of fear. Taking the lead with an entrepreneurial spirit awakens your genius and reconnects you with its power. You do what has to be done; you keep on learning because wisdom is the key to success in your relationship. You claim your role out of natural authority, not out of external authorization. And when time goes by, your entrepreneurial spirit becomes natural, like breathing. Your way to approach resistance, obstacles and challenges will inspire others, including your partner. You feel confident with yourself and the world around you.

The secret of effective leadership in love . . .

is simple to describe. Let your leadership stay a mystery, untouchable for your partner. Leadership in the name of love is like a mist: your partner suspects that there is something but can't catch it. In other words, the art of great leadership in the name of love rests in the power of invisibility. The less your partner notes what's going on, the more you are able to train your leadership skills, test out reactions. The following "Lead-Tactics" will support you in your journey to great leadership in the name of love:

The five "Fresh Eye" lead tactics . . .

will assist you in taking your relationship's lead. Getting back to the sailing boat metaphor, you need to know the starting point in order to set a navigation course to the aspired target.

As a next step you are invited to discover your actual lead habits on ButterflyHabits.com/lead. I encourage you to enhance your personal awareness. After completing the exercise, you are prepared to leverage your actual leadership-personality. Let's have a look at the five essential lead tactics in relationship:

Lead-tactic #1: the power of subtle steps

When you are taking the lead, your personal energy shifts from weakness and helplessness to will and determination. That's perfect and necessary. Nevertheless this kind of energy contains the danger to "overdo" things. Like a pendulum swinging from one extreme to the opposite pole, you tend to exaggerate in your role. The strategy of subtle steps is a secure way to approach your leadership.

Let's assume you have to act on a challenge: your partner doesn't answer your question. Each time you address it there is a change in the conversation's subject.

Ask yourself:

What are other possible options for my reaction?
Rating on a scale from 1 to 3, how intense is their impact?

Scale 3—strong impact model

Send the question by email and ask to schedule a meeting to get it answered.—My *husband acts on emails.* ☺

Scale 2—medium impact model

Prepare his favorite dessert. Before allowing him to eat it, get him to answer the question.—My *husband enjoys eating.*

Scale 1—soft impact model

Taking his hands, look deeply in his eyes and say: "Darling, I need your attention for a question, it's important for me to get it answered."—My *husband responds positively to physical touch.*

Taking the lead in the name of love means to start on scale 1 and only increase—if required.

Lead-tactic #2: the power of motivation

After living abroad for twenty years, my return to Switzerland was a kind of shock. Headlines of newspapers, magazines, advertisements; the manipulation by fear, risks and danger were present everywhere and invaded my being. Security is a highly aspired goal in Switzerland, but at what cost? Studies indicate that people are more animated to take action by fear rather than by motivation. Nevertheless the most important factor is invisible but everyone feels it. It's the energy flowing with those announcements and advertisements. Fear is never the right motivation to act on. Long-term it damages your health and undermines your inner foundation of trust and confidence. "Fresh Eye" tactic #2 emphasizes to take the lead in the name of love, instead in the name of fear and threat. Be patient: the next chapter will offer you insights to identify your partner's motivation buttons, helping you to step out of "destructive" lead habits—shifting and rejuvenating your response patterns.

Lead-tactic #3: the power of flexibility

Is there a difference between leadership style and leadership tactics? Certainly, and it is a crucial one! A leadership style reflects the consistent behavior pattern of a leader. It becomes a habit. And as a survey[14] demonstrated, leadership styles are inefficient, regarding the effect of ever changing environments, situations, and persons involved. Also, the study reveals that different leadership tactics enhance the outcome.

You may experience the same in your partnership. In some relationship challenges a lead style may work, but not in others. Adopting one lead habit makes your partner gets used to it, already anticipating what is going to happen. In contrast, lead tactics are flexible, differ from one situation to another. They are not emotionally driven, instead they are carefully evaluated according to the actual challenge and the partner's emotional state. Therefore, lead tactics are more powerful and create better results. Taking the lead in your relationship efficiently, you are asked to stay flexible. As you know, dinosaurs died from a lack of adaptability.

In challenging situations you mainly act upon emotions, which are usually driven by hidden fears. As a normal process, your reptile brain turns on to protect you. But those occasions require that another part of your brain becomes activated. Instead make it a habit to step out of your emotion to a state of awareness and conscious behavior. Entering that state, you regain control of your emotions, of your words. You reconnect with the power of flexibility in your reactions. The following two Butterfly Habits will assist you in achieving that shift:

Butterfly Habit "close-your-ears countdown"

Disconnect a moment from your partner's words. Concentrate on counting backwards from 10 to 1—quietly inside your head. While counting, inhale deeply between the numbers and then exhale your tension. Remember all the tactics, strategies and skills, you learned from of this book. You are not tolerating misbehavior, neither from your side nor from your partner's side. Remind yourself to take the lead in the name of love.

Butterfly Habit "emotional transformation"

This exercise may be a challenge but you will master it with a little bit of training. It is one of the golden award techniques. Shifting an emotional state is something you already do constantly, but in an unconscious way. Emotions and thoughts are closely connected. Changing consciously to another emotional state shifts your thinking, your whole energy. Suddenly you are able to do and say things, which you could not do/ say before. Remember the 9-dots mystery. You step out of the limiting frame of the 9 dots into a world of new options and possibilities. Start training on an easy level and increase to a more sophisticated one, step by step: e.g., move from being nervous to gratitude, from being angry to taking all with a pinch of humor. Whenever challenges in your partnership show up, shift your emotional state. You will take the lead gracefully and with class.

Lead-tactic #4: the power of reflecting

Another winning tactic is to reflect your inner emotion on your partner. What does this mean exactly? Let's assume you regained an enhancing, emotional state. Starting from this point, you shift your focus from ego to your common love. From the "me" to the "us." You take the lead. In this specific tactic, you reflect your inner balance upon your partner. Also, he owns the potential to find a solution for the challenge you both are facing at that moment. Remember similar situations, which he mastered with excellence, in love. Based on them, ask for his assistance, his wisdom. Perhaps you have to "reflect" several times. Try and observe the results.

I encourage you to anticipate that tactic. Take a quiet moment and remember all the challenges in which your partner has proven emotional strength and responsibility. Take notes to remember them and choose the most appropriate when relying on this tactic.

Lead-tactic #5: the power of contra

Going "Contra" keeps tense moments from igniting into a fight and reflects leadership in the name of love. So what is exactly meant by this tactic? Sharing life with your partner, you share states and levels you possibly aren't consciously aware of.

Believe me, the biggest challenges in partnerships aren't the challenges themselves. The biggest challenge consists in destructive, emotional bonds. If one partner loses the inner, emotional balance, there is a high likelihood that this will affect the other, as well. Remember the example of the 15% increase in feeling greater happiness when being together with a happy person. The same is true in reverse. And this is actually the most critical point if discussions arise in your relationship.

"Dinner is ready!" These few words made him explode and vent his anger. For an hour he has struggled with his computer. He was frustrated, completely out of his inner, emotional balance. Instead of answering from the same level of emotion, I decided to react "Contra." I went over to his office, put my arms around his chest from behind and kissed him gently on the forehead. Then I said: "Darling, I know you work hard, let me help you. Let's disconnect with a nice dinner and regain focus. I know you will then find a solution, as you always do."

"The power of Contra" requires you to limit yourself strictly from emotional imbalances and to transmit your positive, emotional state on to your partner's being. In fact, it is even more powerful in combination with all the other lead tactics, as you note in the "real–life-example" above.

Taking the lead shifts the navigation course of your destiny as well as the destiny of your relationship. You get reconnected with self-confidence and trust. You are the Captain of your dreams. Establish the Butterfly Habit to apply those "fresh-eye-lead-tactics" and enjoy your journey to personal growth.

Chapter 9

Every man owns specific motivation buttons

These are the soul's changes. I don't believe in ageing.
I believe in forever altering one's aspect to the sun.
Hence my optimism.

⌒ Virginia Woolf, English writer,

*His regular medical check-up was listed on the day's sched-
ule. While I cleaned up the table after breakfast, he took a
long, leisurely shower and dressed for the appointment. For
many years we have been friends with the doctor and enjoyed
barbeques and sailing trips together. Before leaving the house,
he approached me, wrapped his arms around my waist and
kissed me tenderly. I said: "Darling, would you ask the doctor
to check your ears? You don't always answer my questions.
Maybe you don't hear well."*

*Two hours later he came home. The medical check-up
revealed that all was in the green range. As I asked him about
his ears he answered:*

My ears are absolutely okay. The doctor wants you to know;
it's not that I cannot hear your questions,
it's that I do not listen to you.

Men and women are different...

that's a fact: from outside to inside. Men's glands e.g., pro-
ducing testosterone, have a radically different effect on their
emotional state and behavior. In addition, studies reveal that
the neurological functions of men's brain are different from
women's, especially with how they receive information and
process it. Men have their language centers in a particular
place of their brains. If this gets hurt, e.g., by accident, a
man loses his ability to speak. But if a women's gets hurt at
the same point of the brain—she will still be able to speak.
Women possess various language centers in their brains . . . to
ensure their speaking abilities? May be this is a demonstration of nature's wisdom, because women need to speak in
order to face the challenges of their lives. You, like me, know
as women we tend to solve our problems while speaking.
But let's talk frankly. Without going deep into neurological
differences between men and women's brains, there exist
gender-based patterns. When a woman connects and com-
municates with a man, she tends to speak and argue from her
point of view, her perception of the world. But honestly, as
woman and man you live in different worlds. What I would
like to emphasize is the importance of being aware of those
differences, at least when challenges in relationships surface.

The risk in labelling your partner . . .

this is the subtle danger you encounter when you start
reading books dealing with relationships. Please remind
yourself regularly: Men are not all the same! Or would you
like to be labeled and get packed in a box together with
millions of other women? You are unique; there exists
no other being like you. You are a singular universe, in
body, mind and soul. You own your unique experience and
wisdom of life and love. In our society we tend to general-
ize—a behavior, which goes hand in hand with ignorance,
injustice and a lack of respect. Gender specific facts are
just like knowing that a plant needs earth and water to
grow. Being aware that there are billions of various plants
growing in deserts, forests and even in the water itself. Be
it sun or shadow, day or night, hot or cold, earth or stone,
plants have different needs to grow. The same applies to
human beings. No person, no man is the same as another.
Diversity ensures reproduction of a strong and resistant
posterity. When reading information about gender differences, please make it a habit to ask yourself the following
questions:

Does my partner reflect those behaviors?
On a scale of 1 to 10, to what degree is this gender-specific
programming part of his personality?

Let's seek to create a win-win situation for both of you
in your marriage. And the subtitle of this book, *Make Your
Honeymoon Last Forever*, emphasizes the aim of this journey—love and happiness for the two of you, equally. This

requires a deep respect for each other regarding the nature of being different. I ask you to apply gender-specific knowledge only and exclusively to enhance your performance, your personal behavior, your communication. Never abuse gender-specific information to blame your partner. Blaming someone about his natural being hurts and will cause damage. Instead always remember the universal law:

What You Focus on Will Grow.

Your partner is unique ...

no other man like him exists in the entire universe. It's no secret: You and I—everyone owns a dark side, hidden inside. We don't like this dark side ourselves. And if someone makes us face our weaknesses, then feelings of anger and frustration arise. Perhaps we have battled that dark side for years to get the weaknesses controlled or eliminated. Unfortunately we tend to turn those negative feelings against the provocateur. True love means being aware of the dark and the light side of your partner. True love also means being aware of the inner fights your partner faces. Do you remember an occasion in which you said something to someone from anger and later regretted it? This is a natural process of "controlling" or "not controlling" those inner, negative patterns. I want you to get the key to supporting your partner, assisting him to reveal his loving side. Both light and dark existed within yourselves when you met the first time. Maybe that daily routine changed priorities, made you neglect the importance of what really counts in your marriage—which are love and respect. When you decided to share your lives, both of you honored the light nature of your beloved, ignoring the dark.

Time is just an illusion. Therefore, I invite you to take a deep breath and reconnect with your honeymoon time. Reconnect with your passion and your love. You have the choice to see the best and unique in your partner at every moment of your life. There exists an invisible connection between both of you. Thoughts and feelings are energies that don't get lost. As you already know: being together with happy people increases one's happiness by 15 percent. The same happens to your spouse. If you fix your thoughts and feelings on your partner's strengths, your energy will permeate all levels of existence: Your being, his being, your lives.

Knowing transmits power . . .

and power comes with responsibility. When you grow in knowledge, you comprehend more about the principles of a happy relationship. This requires that you take responsibility for the common love in your marriage. That doesn't mean that you take care of everything and he has to do nothing. It means that you act from the perspective of a model. On your journey throughout this book I encourage you to start making it a habit to step out of your comfort zone, to unleash the genius within yourself. I want you to get to a point where you love the challenge of compromises. Finding solutions that recognize the voices of both hearts is the most powerful catalyst to love and trust. How many women really do know the silent wishes of their partners? Out of my experience those wishes surface, time after time. Maybe they are tiny, subtle signals—just a look, a comment. Knowing your man's map of his invisible secrets and inner universe requires the commitment to never manipulate. This profound and powerful knowledge is just to enhance and align your personal performance and behavior! Beautiful sea roses may grow out of swamp, but in relationships a solid foundation of love requires purity of trust and confidence. As long as you think, feel, act out of your light side, there's never a danger that you will try to take advantage of your knowledge and act only on your own favor. You are going to reconnect with your partner in a profound way by knowing the wishes and fears hidden in his heart.

The "doctor-episode" at the beginning of this chapter illustrates one thing. Some men are bad listeners and some men are also poor communicators. I strongly recommend that you don't get your partner consciously involved in the analysis of his patterns. Prevent awakening in him the feeling of being a guinea pig. Let's start your journey to his heart, mind and soul!

Your man's unique motivation buttons...

are the key to a loving and happy relationship. Most women don't know that these buttons exist or, if they do, how to apply them. I suggest divorce rates would drastically diminish, if more women knew about the motivation buttons. When women fall in love they usually enter an emotional unbalanced state. They tend to see all through their "rose colored glasses." The glands produce Serotonin in huge masses. You look radiant and younger. Your perspective shifts and focuses nearly entirely on the beloved one. It is a wonderful experience to fall in love and a highly appreciated gift of life. Nevertheless, this state produces blind spots in the perception of the partner. Our mind is a master of illusion. As an example, read the next paragraph:

It'z amzainig waht our mind is albe to cretae. Wehn a raelity sohws up taht deosn't fit the mind's wolrd and rulse; it jsut fugires out a way to mkae it fit. In tihs mometn you are awrae of yuor mind's "cheating" but motlsy tish happnes out of yuor concsiuos obersvaitons. Can you imgane, waht misinertpretatoins arsie out of tihs nautral mind procses? Yuor mind olny is albe to recongize, waht it alraedy knwos.

Everything outside of the personal knowledge and experience bibliotheca get's ignored. And even worse, the human mind is looking to make sense out of what enters its sensual filters. Human mind is unable to recognize the following fact:

Hey, there is something that doesn't fit, there's a blind spot. Maybe I should investigate, if the blind spot is inside of me, rather than outside.

This critical statement can generate a huge shift towards true perception of your partner's personality and being. Your awareness of this automatic mind process defines the starting point to your man's inner map. From this moment, I encourage you to distrust the perceptions of your own mind to make your honeymoon last forever.

Establish the following Butterfly Habits:

- Instead of focusing on what you see, question what you can't see.
- Instead of focusing on what you hear, listen to the unspoken words.
- Instead of focusing on what you feel, try to perceive your partner's feelings.

To identify your man's motivation buttons you need to know his personal "Receptivity Map." Please download your sample for the later exercise on ButterflyHabits.com/map.

The following graph of the map assists your process of exploration and illustrates the various levels of your man's "world."

The dotted circle indicates the fluent transition between inside and outside, what you can't participate in and what you are able to experience.

In the same way as your own inner map, your partner's map starts in his brain. As you know, gender-specific programming is part of a man's brain. Another important factor is his life experience database. All your man's perception of occurrences get stored there, like in an immense library. And I want to emphasize the word "perception" because these are only the filtered results of his mind. Maybe they have no relevance with the true reality. The important point is that all this information conditions his psychological needs, as well as his values. And out of them, he creates expectations, behavior and habits. And those also reflect the physical needs of your partner.

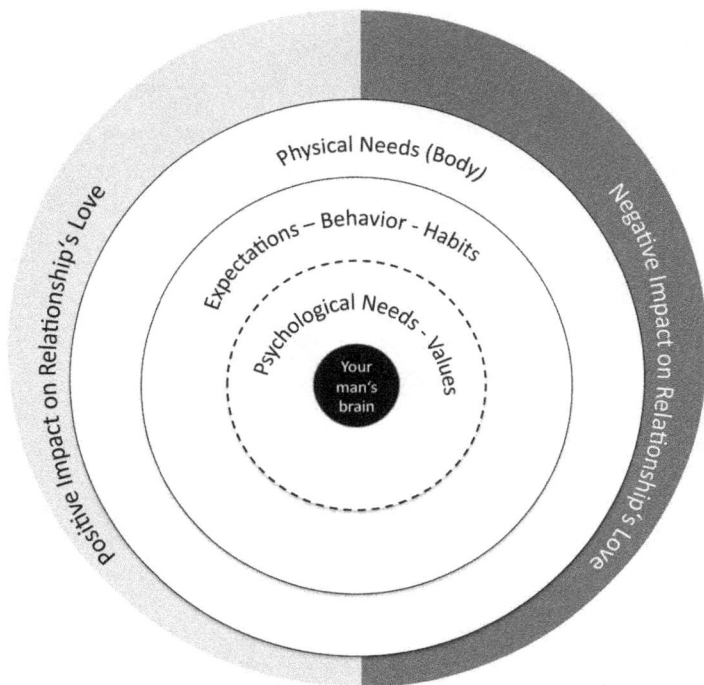

The outer circle of the graph indicates if those patterns nourish your relationships in a positive or negative way.

Let's have a look at your partner's motivation buttons!

The power of fairytales

Did you, like me, enjoy fairytales when you were a child? I couldn't get enough of them. I collected my fairytale books and guarded them like a treasure. When I celebrated my 18th birthday, I thought, it was time to say good-by to my childhood and gave my fairytale books away. Years later, in my work as a speaker, I rediscovered the power of stories.

People just love stories! Stories offer the most elegant way to transmit knowledge and wisdom.

When you grow up, life brings to you your own unique experiences. The way you share stories about them reveals your personal ethics and moral rules, reveals your values—and what is most important to you in life.

It's just a question of listening to how a story gets told. The conclusion, the pronunciation of specific words, the tone of the voice, the feelings transmitted, they all offer deep insights to the storyteller's world. The curtain to a usually invisible world opens to you.

Unfortunately the human brain maintains an idea only for about two minutes. What then gets lost, out of that story, is immensely valuable information about the person, telling it. You lose awareness about deeply hidden, invisible patterns that influence the decisions and behavior of this particular person. I bet you know where this discussion leads you. Correct! The easiest way to get access to your partner's inner world is to listen and remember his stories!

In addition to the "Receptivity Map" an assisting questionnaire will facilitate your investigation. To keep this book handy and slim I "outsourced" it on ButterflyHabits.com/receptivity. Whenever possible, take a silent moment, just you alone, and get connected with the questions and answers. Note them and follow the step-by-step directory. When you have finished all steps continue on to the next paragraph.

Congratulations . . .

You have just built the foundation to make your honeymoon last forever! The "Receptivity Map" is the key to your partner's motivation buttons. Let's have a look at an example to help you understand the brilliant step you took:

Studies reveal that when buying a car, men focus on the power of the engine; while for mothers, the security of their children holds high priority.[15] Imagine yourself being the responsible marketing manager. Would you talk about horsepower in your promotions, when wanting to increase car sales to mothers? Would you try to convince mothers about the importance of engine power? I guess not, because you know you will get confronted with obstacles and results will barely be satisfying.

Switching from professional to personal life, we tend to forget about those triggers that influence decisions and perceptions. Your man's specific values and needs—you now are aware of—determine his receptivity about your information and ideas. From now on you know what the requirements of a win-win-solution will be. And this—finally—is an important factor for harmony in your relationship. Just think one minute about the reverse situation. If your partner recognizes your needs and wishes, you also would feel respected and loved. Sure, sometimes it's not easy to cover both interests equally, but what you have revealed right now will help you to master the challenge of compromises in a "honeymoon way."

Next, I want you to take two additional steps:

- Take a scissor and cut the graph in two parts. Your focus will be exclusively on the part with a positive impact on your relationship.
- The other part of the graph—with the negative impact—you destroy, burn or eliminate right now—to get it out of your world and universe.

Why focus only on the information with positive impact? Your perception creates the reality of your relationship. Your personal attitude is powerful and needs to stay firmly focused on love and respect in your marriage. Therefore, I want you to stay connected only with the motivation patterns of your partner that are related to empowering patterns and feelings. Make it a Butterfly Habit to focus your creativity exclusively on that which generates solutions or makes you overcome challenges in a "honeymoon way."

In a scientific study, professors were provided with erroneous information about the IQ of their students. They perceived the students with low IQ tests as students with a high IQ tests and vice versa. The study revealed, that the students with low IQs (in fact) obtained much higher exam scores than students with high IQs.

Conclusion: The professor's attitude is crucial for a student's school notes.[16]

Establish the Butterfly Habit to sing the daily mantra:

What I see in my loved one, he will become.

In the next chapters you will get deeper insights on how to apply and enhance your new wisdom about your partner's inner map. Let's discover the magic of your man's receptivity map, strengthening the bond of your common love.

Chapter 10

A plan was essential for the flight to the moon; and a plan is essential for a lasting "HoneyMoon"

Far away there in the sunshine are my highest
aspirations. I may not reach them, but I can
look up and see their beauty, believe in them,
and try to follow where they lead.

⌒ Louisa May Alcott, American novelist

*Only three days have passed since I bought the book. The
moment I started to read the first sentence a magic bond was
born. I couldn't stop reading. The book became my shadow.
On every tiny occasion that offered a possibility I headed for
the book. We started the day together and together we went
to bed. The book's magic energized me, stimulated my heart's
dreams. The book became a journey to my true being. The
games and exercises inspired and encouraged me to reach out
for my life's stars. One day I finished another chapter, flipped*

the page and read . . . the next chapter's title "Get a plan." I closed the book. I never read the book to the end.

Everybody's life is jam-packed with plans. Family life, business, fitness, holidays, Christmas; everything is planned. Why? You know the answer. Plans are useful and simplify life. Plans relieve your mind. They assist you to live the moment and free you from future concerns. Plans encourage and motivate. They turn a dream from vision to reality. Plans are guides to ensure that you may reach your goals.

While even your laundry gets a plan, relationships eke out an existence in another dimension. What fool had the idea that relationships require any plan? Planning your wedding, having children, creating a nice home surely are important aspects in a woman's life. Just because you may plan your relationship's package, you still aren't planning the content. Please take note: I absolutely agree that having a marriage and creating a family are unique and crucial decisions. What I am talking about is that woman's relationship plans mostly are limited to those important events in their lives. Instead, I suggest that you see your relationship as a plant. You are encouraged to dig deeper, to protect the health of your love's roots. If you don't care, it will die. High divorce rates all over the world already demonstrate countless relationships competing for the same priority as laundry. Your flower of love needs a plan that waters and nourishes it!

A plan is like an insurance policy

Creating a relationship plan is an ongoing process and a powerful Butterfly Habit; it neither finishes in a dead end nor is it done only once. Planning to protect and nourish your love is an innovative and creative process. It takes some time to convert it into a habit but it will take you a quantum leap forward. A relationship plan constantly encourages you to think about the "relationship fruits" you want to harvest and the seeds those require. Its purpose is to ensure your long-term success in love. A relationship plan takes note of all aspects: challenges, wishes, dreams as well as attaining relationship skills. Your plan will become your mentor. It will be at your side showing you the direction, like a beacon. It will offer you safety and certainty.

A plan makes you preserve your "HoneyMoon"

Do you know the amazing story of how NASA made it possible to land on the moon? Imagine the distance between earth and the goal—thousands of miles! Sure, they made a plan. But what most people are missing is the fact that 99% of the time, NASA's engineers were constantly adjusting the plan.[17] See the situation in your mind's eye: Apollo got launched and all sorts of obstacles and technical challenges happened.

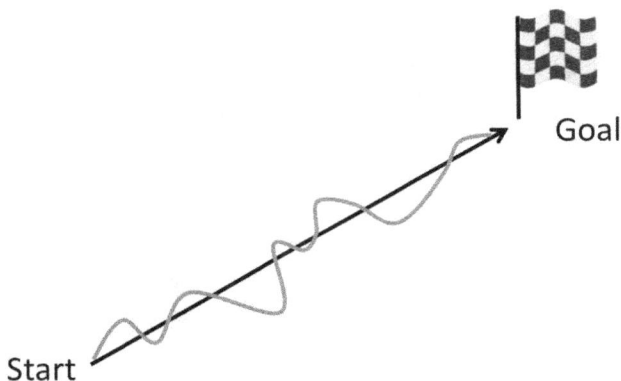

Goal

Start

99 % of time off the track!

How can we expect to work once on a plan and hit the moon or whatever in one shot? A long time ago I was subject of this error. Do you remember the opening story of this chapter? That's why I never finished reading the book. The moment I faced the challenge to get a plan I said to myself that it wouldn't function. And guess why? I never thought about having to adjust the plan. When I got off track, I declared the plan to be useless. I believed that a plan suggested a straight line towards the goal. Imagine what happens instead. The road to success is a line full of tiny curves, made by adjustments.

I would like you to keep this in mind for the rest of your life. Creating your personal relationship's plan is like launching Apollo for your love. To hit "HoneyMoon" and make it last forever, you must have a willingness to make adjustments.

> When it is obvious that the goals cannot be reached,
> don't adjust the goals, adjust the action steps.
>
> ꝏ Confucius

Break it down to finger food

How would you climb Mount Everest? I suggest you don't intend to do it in one swoop. In this case, it's obvious for you to set interim targets, specifically base camps. In daily life, you organize a lot of stuff this way without being consciously aware of that formula. Need a haircut? You find a good hairdresser, then check out where she is located, how to get there, and have an appointment scheduled. This illustrates the various steps to a dazzling hairstyle. However, when facing "big" goals in life, often we focus only on the overwhelming, indomitable mountain peak. Maybe you don't even get started or you give up halfway, feeling like a coward or a failure. The truth is you are neither! You just forgot about the proven formula to set goals successfully. Reaching interim targets while pursuing your dream provides you with a rest to recoup your energy and even more importantly . . . to celebrate your achievements! Your motivation will be inspired and boosted over and over again. Being aware that instead of one "big" step, you take a lot of tiny, single steps. Each step takes you closer to your goal, will release your heart and mind. As you can't eat a cake in one bite, so your relationship's plan needs little tidbits. Start working on your plan with a template to this issue on ButterflyHabits.com/scout.

A plan makes you generate high-quality results

Did you ever have a plan that got smashed in seconds? What happens in such a moment? Maybe you become paralyzed like a rabbit or run around like a headless chicken. In those situations, efficiency tends to be far away, out of your reach. You are required to watch out for a solution and can't afford to explore various options and alternatives. You need a way out, instantly and fast. And guess what happens? Improvisation is the only choice. I don't claim that improvisation is a bad thing. But mostly only second-rate solutions arise. If you would face the same situation on a paper, emotionally balanced, with your mind tapping the world of possibilities, you would create far better quality strategies and solutions for that specific challenge. You would have the time to brainstorm options, to evaluate their strengths and weaknesses and finally rate the best one. Facing the same challenge on paper, you are able to awaken your genius.

Unfortunately you aren't a clairvoyant and therefore don't know the course of the future. But you are able to anticipate all kinds of obstacles and challenges that could thwart your plan. The cliché "An ounce of prevention is better than a pound of cure" also applies to your goal setting. The better you identify potential pitfalls while in the planning process, the better will be your reaction in real-time, generating high-quality results. Make planning a new Butterfly Habit priority and start working with the following process:

Plan your "counter-strategy"

- List inner and outer obstacles that could sabotage your relationship goal;
- Note behind each one your plan on how to overcome it;
- Track the results you attain.

A plan turns relationships extraordinary

As you know the Butterfly Effect says that tiny changes at the beginning cause huge shifts in the final result. The same happens to love in relationship. Let's take advantage of the Butterfly Effect for your relationship's love by planning!

Turn back time and imagine yourself at your wedding day. Dive deeply into this past experience. Perceive this important moment in your life when you gave your vow to the most beloved person in your life. Embrace this gorgeous instance, wholly and fully with all your senses. While in this moment of your life, ask yourself the following questions:

*What do I want my relationship to look like
in the future, ten years later?
How do I want our bond of love to be?
In what ways do I handle relationship challenges
that may turn up?
How do I take care of both of us?
How do I express my love in a daily manner?"*

Observe attentively, listen carefully and feel the emotions. Take note of all these perceptions that show and tell you the magic of your future relationship.

Then imagine yourself sitting on a wonderful site. You are relaxed, happy and feel fulfilled. You are at peace with your mind, body and soul. Now take a piece of paper and develop a plan to protect your relationship's love. You state your personal habits and ethic codes by writing. Ask yourself:

*What will be my daily contribution to myself
and to the loving partner?
How do I make sure to remember the sacred bond
every single day?
How do I ensure to prevent destructive habits?
What rituals will help both of us to handle
challenging situations with excellence?*

Include all those insights in your relationship plan. Don't worry about the fact that perhaps many years have passed since your wedding day. It's still not too late to generate overwhelming shifts. Remember the "Groundhog Day." Each single day offers a new start. The Butterfly Effect is reality and will show the impact even of a tiny shift in your behavior. To suddenly have a relationship plan and to act on behalf of it will transform your life. That's for sure.

Before going ahead with reading, I encourage you to take advantage of this extraordinary opportunity to make your life shift as if by magic . . . or let's say by plan. Take your time to find your answers and note the insights you gain. This is an intimate journey. Do not discuss your insights with others. Each person owns her own story, her own experiences and inner wisdom. You are unique and have to create your unique vision and plan of a loving relationship.

Design your relationship's lifestyle

It's important to create a relationship plan as holistic as possible. It's not just about rules, behaviors, rituals and habits. There is far more to draw in. I am talking about the inner spirit of the two of you. You both have your needs, values and life purpose. It's absolutely crucial to consider those in an appropriate manner in your relationship's plan. Let me reveal another secret for emotional health in a loving partnership. It's not just about you and your partner. In fact you are in a threesome! First, you each are individuals. Then there is the bond of your love. Each one of those three parts needs to be considered in a relationship's plan. Being aware of that, you will initiate a "Honeymoon Revolution," Your love is like a child who needs to be protected. And great protection arises only from individual power. The more balanced and skilled you are, the more solid is the foundation of your relationship's love. Please keep this in mind. Having a well-done plan is like having a car. To reach your destination, you have to drive it!

Often daily life shows up filled with bad spirits and distraction. No wonder so many goals remain just dreams. The Pickle Jar Theory[18] helps you to skip over inner and outer obstacles. In case you don't know: the Pickle Jar Theory isn't a culinary principle. The story behind it is told in various forms. I prefer this one:

Once upon a time there was a guru, teaching his students the mysteries of the universe. One day he put a pickle jar in front of the class and filled it with stones. When no more stones fit in, he asked: "Is the jar full to the brim?" All students said yes. "That's not correct," replied the Guru and added pebbles. When a pebble no longer fit the jar he asked: "Is the jar full to the brim?" The students thought for a moment but said yes again. So the Guru took a sack of sand and filled even the smallest gaps between stones and pebbles. Once again he asked: "Is the jar full to the brim now?" Based on the previous experience, the students showed uncertainty. The guru smiled wisely, took a carafe of water and filled the pickle jar until the water overflowed. "What did you learn from it?" the guru asked the class. One student spoke up and said, "Whenever you think nothing more could fit your daily program, there are always gaps to get it done." The guru replied "No, that's not the lesson. The true lesson is, when you don't put in the jar the important things first, there won't be space for them any more!"

Stay focused and always keep an eye on your daily relationship's plan. I encourage you to consider your insights from the following chapters in your planning. The following ever-omnipresent questions will keep you on track:

Why am I doing this?
In which way does this bring me/us closer to the aim?
How does it relate to personal motivation patterns?
Out of this, how will successes look like?

What's more important: a kiss for your partner or the dishes done? Every day countless opportunities show up to make your honeymoon last forever. Referring to the Butterfly Effect, tiny changes in behavior will create big transformations in your relationship's life. Set priorities according to your most important dream in life. Stay focused and quit bad habits and influences. Make it a Butterfly Habit to keep the vision of your honeymoon alive. There is something very important at stake: your relationship's love. Get started and take advantage of the Relationship's Plan Template on ButterflyHabits.com/planner.

Isn't it astonishing how planning may generate feelings of excitement and joy!

Chapter 11

True communication starts when rash talk stops

So never lose an opportunity of urging a
practical beginning, however small, for it is
wonderful how often in such matters the
mustard-seed germinates and roots itself.

⌁ Florence Nightingale, celebrated British social reformer

*The world turned upside down. I got stuck in the shifting sand
of my life and faced the most overwhelming challenge ever.
Each single day I focused on confidence. My daily task was to
maintain personal balance and fix my eyes on all the tiny, positive moments to gain valuable strength. And suddenly I stood
outside the dimension of my beloved ones. When I was talking
green, they understood red; when I was talking white, they
understood black. My messages didn't get received the way
they were sent. Now, not only the world, but also my communication had turned upside down.*

At this crucial point I started my career as a certified Professional Coach and Master in neuro-linguistic programming. Meanwhile, the quicksand had vanished for many years. My life and relationships returned to being gorgeous and wonderful. What happened? The gate to an invisible world had opened, transforming my perception of communication. Let's pass this gate together in order to offer you some insights I was given.

Evolution ignores human communication

I wonder why evolution seems to have bypassed us humans regarding our communication with one another? All the challenges facing our world demonstrate a great need for improvement in communication between and among people. Perhaps schools could devote time and study to the psychological effect of language? Correct grammar has never saved a relationship! I know that sounds provocative. I want to emphasize the importance of integrating up-to-date knowledge into your personality. Let me tell you a secret. As a matter of fact, evolution didn't ignore us. It just went backwards. In ancient Greece, the art of language, oration and debate enjoyed a high status. Let's have a trip with the time machine to learn principles and habits of a communication style that will ensure your long-term success in love.

"Goodlands" in True Communication

Butterfly Secret #1

It's all about connecting

Do you remember the eye color of a person after having a conversation? Recently I watched an interview with Cindy Crawford about her former husband and film celebrity Richard Gere. She said that Richard didn't sign autographs. Instead he approached his fans and shook their hands, looking into their eyes. This way he created an individual bond to the person's being that an autograph never would have generated. And his fans adored him for it. True communication starts when you connect with your partner, by stepping out of your world and stepping into your partner's world. So what's the biggest challenge in communication with your partner? It may seem astonishing: it's your inner voice.

> I just realized my lips are inside out.
> They should be turned inwards, because I spend
> most of my time talking to myself.
>
> ∽ Jarod Kintz

As long as you listen to your inner voice instead of listening to your partner, exterior communication is non-existent and only an illusion. The required connection for constructive communication doesn't exist.

How can we get rid of this inner distraction? There's a simple way to do it. Your mind just needs brain food. And the best brain food is found in questions. Always remind yourself that the size of the question determines the outcome of the result. Fix on quality!

Challenge your inner voice with brain food

- Which emotion drives my partner?
- Which fear drives my partner?
- Which purpose lies behind those words?
- How can I create a link to his "world?"

Butterfly Secret #2

True communication begins with trust

As emotions drive your destiny, awareness is the key to constructive communication. All the achievements of your "inside-out" journey from chapter 6 make you generate trust in challenging situations. Authenticity, integrity and reliability as part of your personality paint a clear picture and generate in your conversation's partner a feeling of security. Avoid having your fear and doubts on your tongue without speaking openly about those emotions. As a consequence it helps your partner understand the source of your words. This style of communication requires courage and backbone as you open your heart. Whatever will happen in conversation, you are a winner as you act upon your personal integrity. As a person of class and tact, you talk and act with integrity and congruency. And this will generate true communication based on trust in your relationship's life.

Butterfly Secret #3

A personality with class profits from criticism

Being a personality with class means having grown more than others. Your ability to perceive criticism as an opportunity made you learn and progress much more rapidly. Instead of looking for other's faults to make them feel guilty, as a personality with class, you focus on the advantage of criticism. The questions that drive you are as follows:

> *Is this criticism justified?*
> *How can I grow out of it?*
> *What can I gain?*

Being a true personality makes you live in another dimension. You can't be offended by criticism or provocation, as self-awareness and self-esteem make you untouchable. You face criticism actively. You don't judge. Neither do you cultivate resentments, self-reproaches or admit feelings of guilt. As a personality with class, you made it a Butterfly Habit to acknowledge criticism, shift your behavior accordingly and let the past go . . . enhancing the charisma of your person.

Butterfly Secret #4

A true personality owns the crown

Do you remember mind-shift #2 to make each day a "Groundhog Day?" Did you keep that lesson? If not, then skip back to chapter 7. That mind-shift about the concept of failure is crucial as it forms the foundation to handle mistakes and errors. It assists your emotional strength and the intent to focus on growth, instead of arguing, justifying and explaining. As a true personality you reach for the stars. You are a superstar in learning.

Was something said or taken the wrong way? As a personality with class, you own your crown. You provide an explanation from generosity. Your explanation is always an act of self-awareness. No matter how your apology gets received it's an act of personal integrity. And that is what counts.

Grand clean-up challenge

- Make a list of your obvious errors and mistakes in your relationship.
- What did you learn from them?
- How can this improve your personality with class?
- Feel gratitude about them.
- Apologize to your partner, if you have not yet done so.

Butterfly Secret #5

Personalities master the "Fire-Walk"

Do you know the biggest error in communication? People think that communication is a linear process. There is always a previous word or action. That's the principle by which scapegoats get born. But communication isn't linear; communication behaves like a growing helix without having a beginning and an end.[19] It isn't traceable. One person's word follows the other person's word, one person's behavior follows the other person's behavior. The "blind spot" is created by time, as reactions aren't always instantaneous but often delayed. That's the way resentments may influence an actual communication without being detected as the source of disharmony. Therefore each person in the discussion owns the same responsibility. There isn't space for scapegoats any more.

The optimal flow in relationship's communication shows a mutual approximation. You may have your point of view about the issue and he may have his perspective. Maybe, you start from different positions and understand the topic differently. As a personality with class, you focus on common bonds and values. It is crucial to figure out a mutual goal and to answer the question about where to go. As you create the same intention, the primary bond in communication gets established. You turn the me to an us, supporting a loving energy in communication. Sharing your short- and long-term visions, as well as their impact on your relationship, is the take-off point for the talk. Once the common idea or dream is stated, the question—driving the conversation's flow—is about motivations and fears that surface in the two of you.

> People react most to what they perceive
> you are taking away from them.
>
> ⌘ Marcia Reynolds, PsyD, *Wander Woman*

Unbalanced communication mirrors an unbalanced relationship. That's why a personality with class focuses her communication on finding a "balanced" agreement that works for both. Sure, sometimes this requires compromising or making a "deal." Nevertheless it's most important that the outcome satisfies you as well as your partner. A win-win situation reflects the highest triumph in communication.

Balanced Communication

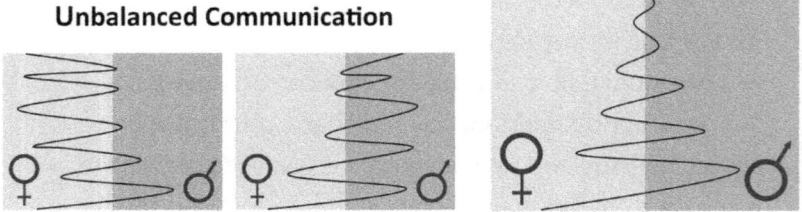

Unbalanced Communication

You may say now: Fanny, theoretically this sounds good, but what do I do when communication sails in stormy waters?

In such communication situations, you face the same challenge as in experiencing a "Fire-Walk." When things heat up, you have to cool down! Then you are challenged to deploy all your communication skills. Remember that awareness and mindfulness are the most powerful communication weapons of a true personality. In addition to making it a Butterfly Habit to reach a common vision, understand personal motivations and recognize fears, there are seven "Fire-Walk hints" to keep an eye on:

Fire-Walk hint #1

"The Power of Ignoring"

Who doesn't remember something one had said earlier, and that one later wished to retract? Mostly that happens because emotions move out of scope. Let me repeat the crucial fact that emotions drive your communication's destiny. When communication heats up, a personality with class needs to be trained to ignore words. To emphasize: we ignore words but not physical abuse. Activate "The Power of Ignoring" by asking yourself questions that truly matter, shift your perspective and calm your emotions. Powerful, insightful questions drive communication back to your relationship's bond and values.

How does what I am going to say support
the purpose of the communication?
Is this relevant now?
In which way will this affect my partner's emotional state?
What are possible side effects?
Will it be said for the best of me or for our relationship's love?

Challenge yourself and prepare your customized, personal questions. When a "Fire-Walk" shows up, you will be ready and confident!

Fire-Walk hint #2
Break bad chains

Accidents that happen in sailing mostly arise from various circumstances. It's not just one thing that drives the course in a dangerous direction. In fact, one little fault connects with another little fault until the big catastrophe happens: the final point of no return. Therefore, it is crucial to anticipate the consequences and to break bad chains. Let's assume that a sailing crew didn't take care to set a safe navigational course and the hull of the boat touches a rock under water, gets damaged. In such a case of urgency the first and most important thing to do is to correct and adjust the navigational course. Secondly one must care about the damage the boat sustained with all options for repair and/

or rescue available at this moment. As the boat's floatability is crucial for the survival of all crewmembers, the focus remains on this challenge until a solution is found. Finally, all involved need to look for the nearest harbor to take care of the boat's damage, shifting the focus to recovering the solid and reliable condition the boat sailed with. Only then will you be able to enjoy the future sailing trips.

In our life relationships, this concept of breaking bad chains also applies. It's critical to anticipate the consequences of words and acts. When communication navigates in stormy waters, the course has to be corrected to save the boat, which in this case is clear communication. When the situation heats up, apply Fire-Walk hint #1 and start cooling it down. Sometimes it's a gentle touch or some simple words that break the bad chain. I encourage you to start figuring out what works best with yourself and your partner. When the communication's course is corrected towards your common values and vision, the healing process may start. Avoid regaining a fast, frenetic daily rhythm again. Make it a Butterfly Habit to take some time to care about the hurts the two of you have suffered until harmony and love are solidly recovered.

Please find some extra techniques on ButterflyHabits. com/chains.

They will provide additional help when sailing in stormy waters or facing a Fire-Walk.

Fire-Walk hint #3

Smart feedback

Offering feedback is a behavior mostly set on autopilot and based on an impulsive reaction. But, woman, you are clever! Connect with your inner potential and start using "mindful feedback." Take advantage of this powerful possibility. Maybe you faced bad experiences in the past. But those only mirrored the results of missing wisdom about Smart Feedback. Actually I worked many years until I discovered this secret. I recommend you apply this principle all the time, not only when facing a "Fire-Walk."

The tricky thing about feedback is to transmit the information without harming the other's being. Unfortunately, in daily life, we become accustomed to focusing on the negative issues. Newspapers, magazines, the whole world seems to transmit negative information. No wonder that there exists a preconditioning and high sensitivity towards criticism.

The only way to overcome one negative comment is with two positive comments. This increases significantly the chance that your partner will face your feedback with an open attitude, as it won't be perceived as aggressive or harming. I encourage you to make this principle of Smart Feedback a Butterfly Habit, as it will enhance the quality and results of your communication. Skip over to my website and check out more insights about Smart Feedback on ButterflyHabits.com/feedback.

Fire-Walk hint #4

Parry with style

What was your mom's communication style? I encourage you to check out the aspects of your personality that mirror her style. As most patterns were incorporated unconsciously, they also get applied this way. In other words, we pattern our parent and don't even realize it.

One day, when cutting vegetables in the kitchen for dinner, I realized that I had adopted an "army style" to communicate with my partner. Strictly speaking communicate is the wrong word, as this would involve both parts. So, without being aware, I assumed a style based on orders and instructions. Military style communication is one way and grounded in giving orders. Military style? It doesn't offer a choice. And choice represents the most important need of a human being. Only choice opens the gate to evaluate options with the personal values of your being. The Military style ignores that aspect completely. This communication style belongs to the army, not in a relationship.

The excessive Peacemaker represents the opposite of the Military style. Generally speaking, being a peacemaker is a most valued role. Nevertheless, there exists a danger you need to be aware of. If you overdo the peacemaker style of communication, you become an excessive Peacemaker. You most likely will end up with deals and compromises that go against your personal integrity. And integrity is your most important treasure. It represents the core of your being.

If you set no limits, if you don't represent your perspective and tend to yield all the time, you enter a dangerous

game. You surrender your values and integrity—you actually shift from peace making to appeasing. Therein rests the
hidden source for the statement:

I don't know what happened. Everything seemed fine
and then suddenly he/she decided to quit our relationship.

It's absolutely critical to maintain personal integrity in
communication. Otherwise, over time frustration builds up
and suddenly explodes uncontrollably. The excessive Peacemaker has to learn to set limits.

The Warrior communication style sets limits all the time,
but . . . doesn't know how to do it in an appropriate way.
The whole being is programmed for survival in a hostile
world. This communication style is fixed on personal integrity. Everything that doesn't match individual rules and
values gets perceived as a personal attack. Expecting one's
partner to mirror 100% of your inner world demonstrates
the weakness of this communication style. In contrast to
the excessive Peacemaker who seeks to please everyone, the
Warrior tends to ignore the interests of others. Imagine the
impact this has on the love in a relationship. There exists
one rule if you discover yourself using aspects of The Warrior communication style: Don't take yourself too seriously!

The Manipulator represents a communication style
that's very difficult to unmask. Words and reactions are
all conditioned to get a specific result. In some way it also
ignores the basic need of free choice. As the Military style
is very obvious, the Manipulator acts undercover in a subtle
way. The Manipulator makes no attempt to find positions
that represent both sides. It's all about achieving one's own

goal. One specific expression of the Manipulator style is to adopt the attitude of a victim. As that is a highly powerful tactic, you can observe it in many relationships. It mirrors a destructive way of communication, not only for the relationship, but also for the person applying this style. By acting out a role of a victim, self-esteem gets damaged and . . . even worse: This role is used as an excuse not to change or do something and that becomes abusive behavior. As a consequence the Manipulator Style inhibits personal growth in communication.

Stop reading for a moment and take your time to detect and unmask your communication style(s)!

Instead of all those destructive communication styles, let me offer you an alternative option. Based on my personal experience, I suggest the Mediator provides the best communication style in a relationship. It offers choice. It respects the integrity of both partners. It supports the evolution of a loving communication. The Mediator reflects the balanced result of all other communication styles. It's about respect as it sets limits in an appropriate way and designs a win-win situation. As a true personality, you act with class and style. Grace and charm leverage your communication skills. You display openness and a willingness to listen, instead of heating up the discussion even more. Parry with style is your communication slogan.

Fire-Walk hint #5

It isn't all about love

We spent some relaxing days with my girlfriend. We hadn't seen each other for months and enjoyed the evening barbecues and day trips together. Unfortunately, in my planning, I forgot a very important issue: the birthday of my mother-in-law. Over the years, celebrating my mother-in-law's birthday with the immediate family gathered was a holy ritual. The encounter took place at her home. My girlfriend's departure was planned the next day to meet some other friends. Thus, the inevitable began as my man asked her, "Could you consider leaving one day early?"

This story illustrates the biggest challenge in relationship's communication between men and women. Women and men perceive situations differently. Genes drive a woman to protect the bonds of the relationship ensuring survival. This genetic aspect highly influences her perception in communication. All issues and topics discussed are connected with the relationship dimension. While a man talks from the problem's content, a woman talks from the relationship even if her words say otherwise. While men figure out the simplest option to handle a problem, women's inner questions are about: Am I respected or not? Does he like me or dislike me? Mostly men talk from results without thinking about the emotional impact of their words while women tend to react upon their emotional state. Make it a Butterfly Habit to ask yourself the following questions when your emotions start heating up:

Over-Arching Question of a "Fire-Walk"

What's the subject of the discussion?
How do I feel in this conversation?
Am I still talking about the problem's content
or is there something else in play?

Fire-Walk hint #6

Emphasis makes the message

There's no doubt that gestures and emotional energy transmit the core of a message. It's not only about what you say, it's even more important how you say it. Voice, emotion and word emphasis are the basics to being effective in communication. As you already have some skills to balance your emotional state, let's have a look at the effect of differently emphasized words. While all people apply it, only a few people make it a habit to apply its powerful impact in communication. Let's challenge your listening and perception:

Speak the following sentences emphasizing the bold word.

- I **appreciate** having your assistance in this issue.
- I appreciate having **your** assistance in this issue.
- I appreciate having your assistance in **this** issue.

Listen, watch and feel the different messages
of the same sentence.

There's no need for further explanation. The word
we choose to accent or emphasize in a sentence speaks

volumes. It invites assumptions and interpretations. And there hides the dangerous terrain, as . . .

Assumptions are the termites of relationships.

 ⌒ Henry Winkler

I encourage you to profit consciously from the power of emphasis. Be aware of the words your partner unconsciously accentuates, as those are the triggers that drive your communication. Trash assumptions and clarify the meaning!

Fire-Walk hint #7
Don't create zombies

One of the most destructive habits in relationship's communication is "Creating Zombies." Instead of living the moment, you reawaken the spirits of the past. That's what I call unfair play in communication. The past has gone. Errors and mistakes have been done and can't get wiped out. A true personality strictly reminds herself to stay connected with the here and now. Experiences and comparisons with ex-partners are No-Goes. A person of class knows that her relationship's future gets created from the present moment, not from the past. What she sows today, she will reap tomorrow. By being aware of that principle, you will keep your mind and words on track and create loving communication in relationship.

Congratulations!

You have completed all hints to master a "Fire-Walk" in relationship's communication. I encourage you to select one hint and practice it until it becomes a Butterfly Habit. Persistency and trust are your most powerful companions on your journey towards true communication. Now, let's discover a classy style of conversation.

Butterfly Secret #7

Personalities of class don't "spam" the partner

As my girlfriend and I drove down the road, the bay lay before us in deepest blue. Nature offered its most precious beauty and caught all of our senses. The smell of the pine trees entered the open car windows. It was one of those moments when words are not necessary. One tries to inhale all the glorious impressions. For half an hour my companion shared each single thought surfacing in her mind. What I most liked about her was an open mind, but in this situation I didn't want to be a part of her brain.

Spamming not only occurs in the inbox of your email account, it also happens in your daily environment. What kind of information do you like to obtain? There's no doubt about the answer: High quality content! Spam information doesn't ask the wishes of the counterpart. In contrast, quality information only arises when the needs of the recipient are considered. Unfortunately you are more aware of the spam you receive in contrast to the spam you transmit. Why is that? The reason lies in the nature of women's brain structure, which differs from that of men. Women solve problems and seek solutions by speaking.

To protect your partner and your relationship from spamming, it's of utmost importance to filter your mind's information. There are thoughts just meant as inner help to find an answer to a challenge, and there are also specific thoughts that need to be shared. There's an inner and an outer dimension. First, always complete your inner conversation until you gain clarity about the issue. Then start sharing your insights with your partner. Remind yourself to be aware of this principle in relationship's communication and start observing its transformational effect.

You want to learn some methods to prevent spamming? Have a look at ButterflyHabits.com/spamming.

Butterfly Secret #8
The art of setting limits

Thousands of porcelain pieces scattered across the floor as the plate broke with a loud crash. It was a Karl Lagerfeld creation: irreplaceable. The situation required an extraordinary reaction, something absolutely out of my normal communication frame, something I'd never done before. I needed to say, "Stop." I needed to set a limit. I needed to break this bad chain!

The Art to setting limits appropriately is a juggling act. It's like turning the volume button of a radio. There are quiet and loud sounds with countless nuances. The irreplaceable plate triggered my loudest sound ever; my quietest sound occurs when I clam up. It's crucial to have more than just one or two sound-levels available, as every situation is different. Stay smart, whatever you decide to do. Keep your emotional state controlled and prevent being thin-skinned. The Art of setting limits demands turning the "Volume button" mindfully. Only then will you be able to observe the effect and adjust your level accordingly. When you throw a plate, as I did, don't do it as an impulsive behavior. You need to know very well what you are doing and which reaction you want to provoke.

Challenge your "Volume button"

- Explore and list your personal "Sound Levels" to set limits.
- Challenge yourself to create and list further variations.
- Note, which "Sound Level" is appropriate to which scenario.

No is the most effective word to set limits. Little children are masters in its application. How often do you say *Yes* and mean *No*? Do you know that such behavior is one of the top reasons for stress? Incongruence with your inner world damages long-term your self-esteem and health. That kind of performance eats away at your happiness in life and relationship. But how to say No in a diplomatic way? You may chose between varieties of tactics. Let's start with the following five:

Tactic #1—Play the damaged record

If you say No, you usually give an additional statement. Remember that specific statement word by word. If your counterpart won't respect your *No* and still bothers you, repeat your statement again. Avoid changing any words. Behave just like a broken record: repeat the line over and over. Play with the sound of your voice. This way you demonstrate consistency and firmness of style.

Tactic #2—Offer something small for something big

Ask yourself, what would be an alternative to offer and listen your inner voice. Then just say:

No, I don't like to . . . but instead I can offer to . . .

This is a conciliatory tactic that I personally like very much. It mirrors my willingness for concessions while respecting my personal integrity.

Tactic #3—Ask for time to think about the request

Request more time for your answer. There are two reasons this tactic demonstrates impact. First, it's often difficult to have an appropriate answer at hand. By being given more time, you may do some soul-searching and look for options to align the issue with your personal integrity. The second point is that most issues have an expiration date and dissolve by themselves. Isn't that great news to start testing this tactic immediately!

Tactic #4—Make a deal

Express the conditions by which you are willing to agree or compromise. What contribution does each one of you offer? What concessions are you both willing to make?

Tactic #5—What if . . .

This tactic is also one of my favorites. Often we just forget to ask: What would happen, if I would say No? This question reflects your need to have a choice. Is the request an order or just a wish? Make it a Butterfly Habit to check out this crucial point. This will make your life much easier and will enhance your partner's awareness about his communication style.

I encourage you to start testing those five power tactics. Please keep in mind to use each tactic about 50 times to establish a natural way of applying it. You will enjoy this process, as you possess many more options to bring into play.

If you feel secure about applying those tactics and would like to get some further ones then skip over to Butterfly-Habits.com/set-limits.

Secret #9

It's all about "timing"

She rented paddle boats. When there was nothing to do, she sat down in the sand next to my sun lounger and we had a chat. I enjoyed listening to the Brazilian sound of her voice. She was a life-experienced woman and had many stories to tell. One day a young woman, obviously a friend of hers, joined us and started complaining about her husband. Many years have passed since then so I have forgotten the topic. What I never forgot was my Brazilian friend's reaction when she said: "Are you crazy to talk this way with a man. First you have to spend a hot night together and then you may properly tell him what you really think!"

The power of timing is an underestimated factor in most relationship communication. In addition to what and how to say something, the when is just as important. What's the best timing strategy? There exist countless options, individually customized to the partner's needs: The Brazil

Strategy of my South American friend is just one of them. Another friend of mine confided that the Wine Strategy works best in her relationship. After dinner she waits until her man feels relaxed with a nice glass of wine. That's his best moment to face challenging conversation. My personal strategy is the Walking Consensus. Moving the body while talking helps to control the flow of emotional energy. If you are having a hot talk, simply walk faster in order to cool down. Select the most appropriate moment to make your partner face your topic openly. Make this your Butterfly Habit. You will see: Even challenging communication will generate magical results.

Challenge your "Timing Strategy"

1. Remember a challenging communication creating a very satisfying result:
   - When did the conversation take place? Weekend, morning, lunch, evening?
   - What was your and your partner's emotional state to start the dialogue?
   - Where did the talk take place?
   - What were you two doing before starting the conversation?
   - What else supported having this constructive communication?

2. Check out the best timing for challenging communication in your relationship:
   - Are you a power woman when starting the day, while your partner only hours later is in top form?

- What are the differences and similarities in your bio-rhythms?
- How do you keep in mind your two bio-rhythms before starting a discussion?

"What Timing Strategy did you discover?"

Badlands in Communication

When I listen to political broadcasts, I am always aware of the huge gaps in the knowledge of professionals' communication. How can you expect smart communications skills from yourself as even politicians themselves show shortcomings? Learning and growing is a true personality's nature. Being aware that there is always some wisdom to leverage your life quality sensitizes your perception. Since it takes about two months until a new habit is established, let's tear down the cornerstones of Badlands communication. There exist specific words that generate a sizzling effect in communication. Especially if you use them during a Fire-Walk conversation, you risk heating up the discussion even more.

Badlands cornerstone

MUST

This simple word ignores a human's need of having a choice; it denies liberty. "Must" is an order and reflects an energy which allows no contradiction. The crazy thing is that you don't just use this word in your outer communication: you also apply it for yourself. In chapter 6 you learned to shift your life and relationship's world from inside out. The same happens with all the Badlands cornerstones. To get rid of them you are challenged to educate your inner voice. The way you talk to yourself is the way you talk to your partner. Make it a Butterfly Habit to take care of yourself, as you then also take care of your relationship!

Badlands cornerstone

SHOULD

This word psychologically shows a softer impact but still goes along with a negative emotional charge. Applying this word in daily communication you ignore your inner No. You despise your personal integrity and damage your self-determination. Start listening attentively to your words and the words your partner uses. Assist him in acting congruent with his inner integrity. He'll love you for this.

Challenge your inner Must and Should

Feel the emotional effect of the following sentences:
- I must call my mother! ~ Obligation
- I should call my mother ~ Guilt
- I will call my mother! ~ Decision
- I could call my mother! ~ Choice
- I want to call my mother! ~ Wish

Badlands cornerstone

Always—Never—Nobody—All

All Men are equal. Maybe in the act of creation or in the eyes of the universe but in plain, down to earth, human reality, this saying is a lie and you know this. The delicate matter about generalizations is their impact on mind and soul. They cause harm. Surely you've had some personal experiences. Nevertheless these words are part of your daily communication—inside and outside—and spread poison in your life and relationship. Generalizations are like weeds. They need to be controlled in order not to take over your conversation. Do you have a garden? Then you know the effort it requires to get rid of weeds. Strategy and persistence are the "Dream Team" to clean up with those bad habits. First, fix one generalization you are used to applying in conversations by identifying it and getting rid of it. When you have integrated the new thought, concept/word in your language, then replace some more. Cool down and note the sovereign power of this communication style!

Soften your generalizations

All / most / some
Never / seldom
Nobody / few
Always / mostly / often

Badlands cornerstone

B U T

"But" is the riskiest word in your daily communication. What causes harm is not the word itself. The danger consists in its positioning in a sentence. "But" applied the wrong way acts as eradicator. Everything you said before this word gets deleted and doesn't exist anymore . . .

> *You look pretty with this new haircut,*
> *but the color doesn't match very well.*
> *I love you, but you forgot my birthday.*
> *I enjoyed the dinner, but the wine was awful.*

Can you imagine how many misunderstandings arise from the word "but" in relationship's communication? They are countless. "But" is a word in your language, set on auto-pilot. Most people are not aware of its destructive impact and wonder why their results in conversation are poor. Instead of searching some source within their language, they see the problem only in their partner's behavior. The word "but" may be a powerful element in communication when applied the right way. It may generate motivation, trust and self-esteem, as it is active in your inner and outer conversations . . .

> *You lost your sunglasses, but you found a new friend.*
> *Your performance was not outstanding,*
> *but I admire your courage to do it.*
> *I still need to lose some weight, but I look great in these jeans.*
> *I missed the target, but I have learned a lot.*

"But" has a big impact on the emotional state. The good news is . . . being aware of this word in communication's flow: especially when you realize that your counterpart applies it the wrong, destructive way. As you are aware of his "fault," you switch the message in your mind. Instead of a negative emotional impact, you may generate for yourself a constructive feedback. This simple strategy will leverage your communication to star performance!

Keep leading your journey to a great communication and take advantage of the following exercise on a daily base. Make it a new Butterfly Habit. As far as possible win your partner as an ally. With both of you becoming aware of Badlands communication, you will boost the enjoyable changes in your relationship.

Challenge your Badlands

- Your outer communication reflects your inner voice.
- Repeat silently sentences of the conversation, word for word.
- What Badlands cornerstones surface?
- Readjust your/his message appropriately.

Remember the Badlands in Communication. Celebrate your attainments and always stay connected with the following quote:

> Nothing is impossible, the word itself says,
> "I'm possible!"
>
> ⌐ Audrey Hepburn

A Remembering of "Goodlands" in Communication

- It's all about connecting
- True communication begins with trust
- A personality with class profits from criticism
- A true personality owns the crown
- Personalities master the "Fire-Walk"
- The Power of Ignoring
- Break bad Chains
- Smart Feedback
- Parry with Style
- It isn't all about love
- Emphasis makes the message
- Don't create Zombies
- Personalities of class don't spam
- The Art of setting Limits
- It's all about "Timing"

Chapter 12

The Butterfly Effect is an omni-present power in love

Be less curious about people and
more curious about ideas.

∽ Marie Curie, Nobel Prize winner and physicist

It was one of those beautiful evenings in spring. Nature exploded in vibrant colours, and smells. The naked forest started to dress up in boundless shades of green. Finally the winter's cold was beaten. For two weeks we had been enjoying evening walks after work. It was a wonderful routine to leave daily tasks behind and flip the switch from career to personal life: from them to us. I enjoyed moving my body, purifying my mind with the gentle wind and listening to birds sing. After a long winter it was funny to see the cows, expressing their pleasure by romping around in the meadows. We were on our way home walking hand in hand on the sidewalk along the busy village street—I on the side closer to the road. Without saying a word, he suddenly changed our position and took my other hand, protecting me from the cars like a precious treasure.

As a house is constructed brick by brick, love in a relationship gets expressed in countless small things. But often we overlook them, aren't aware of them. After years, our perception tends to shift to all the things that we dislike about our partner. As women, do we have a predisposition to see the glass half empty instead of the half full?

The fact is that the male brain selects information differently from the female brain. Man's brain especially forgets negative experiences. Not so the woman's brain. Five- or six-year-old girls remember criticisms, offenses and failure much longer than boys.[13] This generates negative influences in women's self-esteem as well as their relationships. Unfortunately you can't just have your woman brain replaced but . . . the good news is, you are able to recondition it. Persistency is the key that makes your brain filter and process information differently. Persistency will boost your happiness in love.

Persistency is available for free at any moment for everybody, and also for you. And as the Butterfly Effect is a fact, isn't it motivating to know that just a little shift in your thoughts can generate impressive changes in your life and relationship? Are you as excited about this as I am? When I discovered the universal law of the Butterfly Effect and started using it, astonishing things happened in my life. Maybe my first little shift created subtly better results. But . . . and at this point of the book I choose to write again a big "BUT" . . . after generating several little shifts my relationship turned exponentially better. The transformation not only takes place in you, it also affects your partner. Imagine a wave of energy changing the sense of the world's dimension around you. What I am sharing with you is teachable; not just some nice thought, feel good construct. It actually saved the harmony in my personal relationship with my parents. And this universal law of the Butterfly Effect can have a powerful impact in your life and partnership too. Along your journey in being a person of class, you begin tuning the sensitivity of your perception, just like a musician is tuning his instrument. When you increase your ability to truly "see," you become aware of opportunities presenting themselves regularly in your daily life to enhance your relationship. Your creativity in leveraging small habits and daily occurrences will increase. I am excited to share with you the following Butterfly Habits, which are my personal suggestions and the ones I use in my life. Try them. Don't hesitate to expand them and personalize them to make them your own. Now, let's open the gate to new small habits that assist in shifting you to happiness in love.

Butterfly Habit

Don't do, what you don't want your man to do

This principle is simple as well as logical, but we forget about it. As your woman's brain makes you focus on the negative, guess what happens? Your relationship's world tends to become more unsatisfactory. He doesn't take out the garbage. His dirty, stinky jogging shoes sit in the main entrance of your home. He has yet to clean out and wash the car. You start nagging. Okay, those situations do call for action. But use the communication style I shared with you in the previous chapter!

Nagging, grumbling, and criticizing become an uncon-scious habit. I have observed that many relationships suffer from this behavior. Who wants to be criticized for every little thing not done perfectly? When I faced the challenge to quit this bad habit, I asked for assistance of my beloved one. Nagging and criticizing may become such a part of who we are that we are unconscious of doing it. We need to have some coaches in the guise of family and friends to help us see what we are doing. This Butterfly Habit isn't just about nagging your partner. It's a powerful perspective to keep you on track whenever challenging situations show up in your relationship.

Butterfly Habit
Always think of Rome

Haven't we all heard some version of this story:

The lady of the house was preparing a braised leg of lamb when the man of the house entered the kitchen. Watching her cut the bone shorter, he asked: "Darling, why do you cut this bone?" The lady of the house answered: "Because a delicious braised lamb leg has to be done this way. My grandma and my mother always prepared it this way." The man of the house wasn't persuaded by that answer and called his mother in law. "Yes," she said. "That is how I always prepared mine because that is how my mother prepared hers." Her answer did not satisfy his curiosity. Therefore he visited his wife's grandma. He asked her about preparing the leg of lamb and why she cut the bone. *Grandmother laughed and said: "In the past we used to have much smaller pots. I cut the bone so the lamb would fit in the pot. With today's bigger pots, there's no reason to keep on doing that."* (Source unknown)

Do you have your own particular approach to housekeeping? These habits have been instilled in you. They are an automatic behavior and as in the previous story, you tend not to question them. Maybe you are set on autopilot and follow them, as a puppet marionette must obey its strings. As every person has a unique way of handling things, differences emerge on how to do routine chores. Then comes the discussion about whose way is right. From childhood I was taught to organize my stuff. Each weekend my mother checked my wardrobe and desk drawers. If I had everything well organized, a delicious piece of chocolate was my reward. Imagine the challenge my man was facing. I didn't like any stuff lying around. Finally, one day I recognized my inability to sit still and talk with my husband after enjoying dinner. I believed I had to clear the table immediately. My behavior mirrored my addiction. Little by little I started my "detoxification." I stayed seated one minute longer at the table, trying to ignore all the dirty dishes calling for action, and fixing my attentiveness on my partner. Then, minute by minute I improved the challenge. Today I enjoy dinner, free from my inner obligation to clean up the table immediately. Also instead of having all shoes properly lined up, I offered my husband a big basket to put his shoes in. I developed inventiveness in terms of ordered chaos. All the small changes simplified my life significantly and strengthened the harmony in our relationship.

Challenge your habits

List all the things you and your partner differ about. Then work to discover out-of-the-box solutions that simplify your life and increase your partner's happiness.

No idea about an issue on your list? Skip over to my blog and get some inspiration to boost your creativity. Remember, there's always a gap to universal wisdom.

All roads lead to Rome . . .

⌒ Jean De La Fontaine, *Le Juge Arbitre, Fable XII*

Butterfly Habit

Mix lifestyles

If you would paint a picture of your personality in the terms of flowers, would you be an elegant rose with thorns, a playful daisy or a wild dandelion? That simple question could create a bouquet of flowers. Your personality can't be described in one flower or one term. Your personality owns a variety of facets. The picture you paint will not have only one single color. In everyday routine, we tend to ignore our true being, who we really are. As a consequence our relationship's life becomes colorless. Recall every aspect of your personality: voice, dress, dreams and life style. When you start to re-awaken your "colors," your inner beauty surfaces and your relationship starts to flourish again.

Challenge your relationship lifestyle

- List all facets of your personality: Are you an underground hippie, adventurer, artist, seductress, dancer, storyteller, astronomer, motivator . . . ?

- When or where in your life did you get those aspects of yourself fully expressed?
- How did you feel, talk, look, think?
- In what ways can this aspect of your personality enrich your life style?
- How can it nourish your relationship's love?

Butterfly Habit

Ignore weakness and promote strength

Imagine a highly talented piano player. Would it make sense to teach him to play a violin? What level of mastery could he attain? How would this affect his motivation? If the pianist were to continue to invest the same energy in playing the piano, what would be the result? This butterfly shift isn't about making music. Studies on work efficiency indicate that promoting strengths instead of weaknesses generates a significantly better outcome. The same applies to your relationship. Let him contribute what he loves to do. Does he like to handle the tax return? Take advantage of it! Does he like to go for a spin? Appoint him to be responsible for the disposal of waste paper and glass for recycling! He enjoys having a beer with some friends? Hand him, with a gentle kiss, the shopping list for the supermarket near the local restaurant or bar where he likes to meet his friends! Whenever possible connect tasks with a positive anchor. This is the best motivation to have him participate in the daily tasks. Of course, this also applies to you. Are there some tasks you both don't like? What could you do about them? Start your free "Strengths/Weaknesses Challenge" on ButterflyHabits.com/strengths.

Butterfly Habit

Make friends with the subconscious mind

Do you like red sweaters? Maybe you have been influenced by the following story:

A professor wanted to demonstrate to his students the power of the subconscious mind. He asked the class to establish a new routine. Every time somebody showed up with a red shirt or sweater, the students had to compliment that person on her/ his attractive appearance. After only a few days, the presence of red sweaters and shirts in the school increased significantly. Based on their new wisdom, the students decided to influence the professor's subconscious mind. Each time the professor lectured from the left side of the classroom, the students reacted with disinterest and ignored him. The moment he taught from the right side of the classroom, the students showed motivation and passion for his issues.

Guess what happened! The professor taught mainly from the right side of the room until the students revealed the secret test.

I want you to become aware of the power of motivation and attentiveness. Every experience generates an anchor inside the person and the subconscious mind reacts on it. Instead of your "nagging habit" continuing to control you, imagine installing this new, positive and productive habit. You will trigger magic shifts in your love and relationship. Please handle this knowledge wisely for the best outcome for both of you!

Butterfly Habit

Own your emotions and clean up the canvas of your life

Can you imagine a world in which constant evaluating, judging, and comparing no longer existed? All your expectations and disappointments would vanish in another dimension. Living the moment would be a constant part of your being. Instead, resentments from the past often influence the future. We build walls around ourselves to keep from being hurt or challenged or judged. Those walls prevent us from reaching out for the amazing possibilities outside. Forgiveness can initiate a powerful shift in life and relationship. Forgiveness helps us to let go of resentments. But how do we face the challenge of forgiveness if the heart is filled with anger and pain? I also struggled with this paradox. Then I finally found help in two simple questions:

What must the person do or say so that I am able to forgive?
Imagine the person having done or said what was needed:
Do I really forgive completely?

When I recognized that the person for whom I held resentment had no way to receive forgiveness, the perception of the problem changed. I noticed that the dilemma wasn't any more the person. The dilemma was inside me. I had to seek a way out. I would not accept any more the agony of my mind and emotion. Sometimes forgiveness isn't a question of others. Sometimes liberation is possible only by forgiving ourselves: for ignoring signals, demonstrating a lack of integrity, refusing to assume responsibility and more. Closeness in a relationship may generate injuries, as we all are humans. As a caring, perceptive partner recognize that it is critical to eliminate every small pebble of injury with a ritual of inner and outer forgiveness to clean up the canvas of love in your relationship's life. You not only will liberate your partner, you also will free yourself from unnecessary burdens.

Butterfly Habit
Dance "A Little Bit of Mambo Number 5"

Do you know the million bestseller Mambo N° 5 from Lou Bega? It was the summer hit just a year before the turn of the millennium. Take a little moment and skip over to YouTube to get connected with the song's message. When you listen to the refrain, you will know what this next butterfly shift will be about:

> A little bit of Monica in my life
> A little bit of Erica by my side
> A little bit of Rita's all I need
> A little bit of Tina's what I see
> A little bit of Sandra in the sun
> A little bit of Mary all night long
> A little bit of Jessica here I am
> A little bit of you makes me your man

∽ From *MAMBO NO. 5 (A LITTLE BIT OF. . .)*
by Prado/Bega/Zippy[23]

Men are hunters. To ignore this fact as a woman can get you in trouble. This song text will not tell you to ignore your true being. Quite the contrary! Once again I challenge you to get in touch with all facets of your individuality. Knowing yourself and being that "you" allows you to manifest the highest level of integrity. You are Monica, Erica, Rita, Tina, Sandra, Mary and Jessica. You are loving, crazy, smart, great, clever, sexy, cool . . . and an amazing woman. Let all those aspects of your female personality dance. Take advantage of the power of surprise and start enjoying the fruits of the liberation of your inner being. You will emit an energy of irresistibility on all persons, not just your man. I discovered that fascinating others resulted in fascinating him. Always stay connected with a pure energy. Keep in mind: you do not want to provoke your partner's jealousy. Your intent is to stimulate his love for you.

Butterfly Habit

Treat him like a lover

Do you remember childhood and hunting for eggs mysteriously hidden everywhere in house and garden at Easter? Curiosity and secrets are a most powerful link. When falling in love, you were curious to discover all about your partner and surely you shared some delicate secrets as well. As years have passed, curiosity and secrets have gone into hibernation. Your partner also possesses numerous, amazing traits. I would like you to reawaken the lover within him. I am not talking about sex—not yet. I want to emphasize the power of curiosity and secrets to rekindle the spark in your relationship. Start playing the "Secret Game:" hidden love notes, a secret tenderness under the table when invited to dinner, a seductive glance during the barbecue with friends. Play every card in your hand. There are plenty of opportunities to renew flirting. Maybe your partner gets irritated at the beginning, but . . . trust me, men love to play games and can't resist the temptation of secrets and surprises.

Butterfly Habit

Treat him like a little boy

Hand in hand we walked along the beach while the sun was slowly setting at the horizon. As the heat of the day kept people in their homes, now at this late hour many families with children enjoyed the sea. Looking at the kids playing in the sand, he suddenly said: "I have to borrow my friend's child to get official permission to build my own sand castle."

One important thing I learned in relationship is that there is always a little boy in a man: cheeky and playful. Having fun, enjoying life, doing something out of character stimulates happiness and love in your relationship. Our daily responsibilities and tasks cause us to forget the pleasures of life. We grow too serious about everything. Scientific studies show that the "humor muscle" degenerates on the way to adulthood. While we laughed as a child every day about 400 times, we confine the muscle of humor as an adult to sad 15 times a day[20] But laughing is healthy. It releases stress and generates happiness hormones. When was the last time you did something crazy and spontaneous like drawing him into the shower? What do you think about first . . . the pleasure or the mess of his wet clothes? Challenge your craziness and spontaneity as a Butterfly Habit to boost happiness and fun in your relationship. There are countless opportunities to start your new practice. Share your journey to craziness and join my blog to inspire others.

Butterfly Habit

Refresh the magic of touch

For years, her weekly massage resulted in an intimate friendship. Enjoying her relaxing treatments, we used to share our stories of daily life. She had been single for two years. "Do you know what I miss the most?" she asked. "The cuddling, the hugs and kisses."

We know there are various types of kisses: a charming kiss on the hand, a passionate French kiss or an Eskimo kiss. Kissing is the expression of romance, affection and love. Statistics show that French couples kiss each other an average of 7 times per day, while Japanese couples only share about ½ kiss per day. This means just one kiss each second day! How often do you kiss your partner? Scientific studies also reveal that kissing burns up to 27–28 calories! Even dentists say that kissing makes for healthy teeth and lips. Kissing is the fastest and cheapest beauty booster ever! Get your creativity started and enjoy this journey to romance. Want to know more about the science of kissing? Skip over to ButterflyHabits.com/kiss-science.

Kiss Challenge

- When your partner leaves home for work, or on an errand, or for any reason, kiss him as if this would be your last kiss ever
- When your partner comes home, kiss him as if he is the grandest thing that enters your life right now.

Kisses also release the sexual bond to make love. And here, we have finally arrived at the hottest issue of this book: Sex, the most beautiful minor matter in the world.

> The main problem in marriage is that for a man
> sex is like eating. If the man is hungry and can't
> get to a fancy French restaurant,
> he goes to the hot dog stand. For a woman,
> what is important is love and romance.
>
> ∽ Joan Fontaine

Do you remember the beginning of your love, the passion and tenderness, the need to touch and explore each other? Have you turned the page of this chapter or is it still open in your relationship? The nature of men can't be beaten by logic. It is an inborn instinct in every male of this planet to ensure survival. It is as sure as the course of the stars. And . . . sex makes life beautiful! It releases stress and rejuvenates. But is it possible for a woman to become sensual instantly? It is a fact that you can train your passion as any muscle of your body. To rekindle your inner fire and desire get your mind congruent with your emotion. Repeatedly think, "I love to have sex!" or remember your "first time" and feel the magic that happens in your body. Making love is the most intimate bond between a man and a woman.

Butterfly Habit

Claim your queendom of love

A relationship needs a pure environment to make love grow. Quantum physics prove that everything is energy: beginning with the elements of atoms and on to music, people, emotions, thoughts, and talks—everything. Your relationship's vibrancy is influenced all the time. That's the reason why a quarrelling couple may poison your relationship's harmony and cause you to start quarrelling, too. Become aware of those destructive influences and eliminate them. Start a ritual of having an emotional rating of your personal contacts with people, together with your partner to erase toxic influences. This also enhances his awareness about those harming "ghosts" of our relationship's love.

> If you want to be smart, surround yourself
> with people who are smarter than you.
>
> ⌐ Source unknown

Reviewing the Butterfly Habits to skip the "Seven-Year-Itch":

- Don't do what you don't want your man to do
- Always think of Rome
- Mix life styles
- Ignore weakness and promote strength
- Make friends with the subconscious mind

- Own your emotions and clean up the canvas
- Dance "A Little Bit of Mambo Number 5"
- Treat him like a lover
- Treat him like a little boy
- Refresh the magic of touch
- Claim your queendom of love

Part Three

The dot on the "i"

Chapter 13

Having a mentor is hitching
your love to a star

We have all a better guide in ourselves, if we would
attend to it, than any other person can be.

⌐ Jane Austen, novelist

Ships' sirens tore me from sleep and I heard the incessant humming of the wind in the wires and the mast. Something was wrong. I put my head out of the hatch cover. It was a stormy night and the spray was dancing and splashing everywhere. Darkness everywhere, without a moon or any stars. Just the anchor lights of the other boats let me know that I wasn't alone. And then I realized: My boat was about to run aground! The worst nightmare of every sailor had come true. I started the engine and tried to raise the anchor. But Poseidon, god of the sea, was stronger. Suddenly he stood at my side like a guardian angel: a stranger with a French accent. He helped me to bring my boat to safety and then . . . disappeared back into the darkness of the night.

Reframe your mindset of help

Are you a lonely hunter? Do you love to figure out things on your own? If so, you will know how to attain the most from this book. I love being a lonely hunter. I learned juggling, Hatha Yoga and even Spanish without attending any classes or working with a teacher. Sure, that's not the quickest way but a most enjoyable way. To figure out things on our own supports the feeling of independence. As long as that is the reason for not asking for help it is okay. However, many people perceive asking for assistance as a symbol of weakness. To rely on someone else is like confessing to being unable to learn on one's own. That kind of thinking is a bit schizophrenic: even as top athletes, movie Stars and managers consider having a professional coach at their side as mandatory to enhancing their results. They know . . .

Two brains do not add up, but multiply!

What drives you to play Superwoman, even if you don't have supernatural powers? Do you think that's the only way to get things done or are you looking for recognition? Whatever the reasons are, it is crucial to be aware of what keeps you from asking for support. Do you like to give gifts or offer compliments, but when given the same from others you feel uncomfortable? In this case "Giving is better than receiving" may be a mindset limiting you; making you unable to feel the same joy, like others. I want you to clearly understand, right now, that giving and receiving is the same as the interplay between ebb and flow, day and night. The law of nature always seeks balance in all elements of creation. If you change the rules of your inner world, you will open a gate to other options in life. Having options allows for more choices: The source for personal well-being and optimal inner alignment.

Challenge your mindset of help

- How do you feel about asking for help?
- What do you think about yourself when asking for help?
- What does your inner voice tell you when you intend to ask for assistance?
- If you benefitted from having support, how may your personal awareness change?
- If you would enjoy some support, how would your relationship benefit?
- If you would enjoy some support, what would be the impact on your motivation?
- What do you think it would be like to have someone of trust assisting you?

Free your head and heart

How can you reawaken magic in your relationship and stay on track with the insights you gained out of this book? To make love grow you are challenged to generate more leeway and declare your relationship a priority in life. Make it a habit to chase away the dark clouds of obligation in order to brighten your love's sky, to free your head and heart. A simple yet profound principle states:

The more hands help you to carry, the easier it will be for you.

There is a variety of possibilities for assistance you can take advantage of, many of which you are not aware. In daily life you obey your habits like a robot. As long as you think that something can be done only one way, the door to new possibilities remains closed. Let's have a view behind this door and discover the various options of assistance and help waiting for you.

The inner circle of assistance: collaborators, teams, and alliances

Your partner, family, children, friends, neighbors, colleagues in your personal, and business life create a huge network of contacts that can be part of your world. They all represent an option to make your relationship grow happy, to free your head and heart. Each one of them stands for a possibility to learn. Each one of them is a master challenging your skills.

As studies[11] show that a lack of communication is one of the top factors for broken relationships I encourage you to use the knowledge you gained in the previous chapters. Best of all: you are the Game Maker. You may make your skills grow without telling others. Or you may let them know that they are welcome as part of your personal communication training. It's up to you. Whatever you decide, I encourage you to involve others in your journey and to encourage them to be collaborators. Don't tell them that you are working on your relationship's love. Keep it a secret. Just tell them that you would appreciate their assistance as mentors in enhancing your personal communication skills. Believe me, people feel honored to get involved this way and perceive it as proof of your trust in them. As an example, ask your partner for assistance to increase your awareness about Badland patterns. Be a model! Teach him the rules of constructive feedback. Make him your coach for personal growth. As certain as $A+B=C$, so also your relationship will change. By changing yourself, you already change one element of that formula. Results will turn up. When he starts enjoying this "journey," he will be open also to further ideas for brightening your love's sky.

The Inner Circle is also a great source to gain flexibility with daily duties. When tasks and rules govern your daily life with strict regimentation, you tend to lack energy and motivation. But you need them to stay focused on your plan, your training of awareness for relationship's love. Daily tasks done by a team would simplify your life. Beside your job, which tasks take precious time away from your relationship? Children's transports, glass and waste paper disposal, food purchases?

A variety of tasks could be shared with like-minded people. As an example, my girlfriend used to drive to a remote farm to buy organic fruits and vegetable every week. She always lost half a day's time to accomplish this task. She organized a group of six like-minded neighbors and friends. Now she faces that duty only once every six weeks instead of every week. Isn't this an elegant way to gain time to invest in your relationship goals! Integrate the Butterfly Habit to look out for daily duties that would be suitable for the team idea. Discuss options with the inner circle of your world since you know that brains don't just add up, they multiply.

What is the most frequently asked question when your anniversary is around the corner? A girlfriend of mine is an expert in taking advantage of the question: What do you want for your birthday? Is it an hour together declaring war on the weeds in her garden, or enjoying an afternoon together for her home's spring-cleaning. She is a genius in creating wishes that combine win-win situations with fun. Additionally she became an event specialist in private life. After the renovation of the windows of her house, she invited all friends to a barbecue and organized games where each loser had to clean a window. Isn't this an amazing way to generate alliance! Make my girlfriend your model. Create your birthday list and fun events generating more precious time for your love.

The outer circle of assistance: outsourcing

Did you notice that happy persons are irresistible? Think about Heidi Klum and Cameron Diaz. Their smiles spread magic. Wouldn't you like to spend your time with them, too? Dancing with your daily tasks makes life easier, generates better energy and causes you to smile. However, there may be duties that you as well as your partner dislike doing. Those are the ones to keep an eye on as they might weaken your relationship's foundation. If you are not able to reach a mutually satisfying resolution on those duties, then outsourcing may be another option of assistance. Did you ever evaluate the costs of services countless Solo entrepreneurs are offering for help in the household? Look closely at the daily and weekly routines and rituals you engage in and consider how they might be stealing valuable time of togetherness! What may add most assistance and support to your relationship's love? Under what conditions may this

kind of assistance be an affordable investment in your love?
Does the possibility exist to barter? To arrange a kind of
deal or exchange of skills? Think about the values you both
could offer.

Challenge your assistance by outsourcing

- What are the duties and tasks you and your partner
  dislike to do?
- Rating these from 1 to 10 (1 represents the most dis-
  liked task), what is your rating?
- Are those duties and tasks doable by businesses or
  retired workers?
- What outsourcing would add most value to your relationship's harmony?
- When this task gets outsourced: What would you and/
  or your partner do for your relationship's love instead?

Love's silver lining and the crucial point to request an expert's assistance

Getting married or obtaining a divorce is a most important
decision for women; all kind of people are prepared to offer
advice from the best of their intentions. They may protect
you, encourage you or envy you secretly. Whatever the hidden purpose may be, you alone will bear the consequences
of your decision. Advices that others offer reflect their
experiences and life rules and are just a mirror of their inner
worlds: not yours. Your inner world is unique and the best of
all solutions, all answers come from within yourself. The best
help you can expect is from someone who makes you see your

inner world, who makes you hear your inner voice and makes you clarify the essence of your contrasting emotions.

When the moment arises that you don't know where to go or what to do, you are behaving like a prisoner in a maze. You move forward and backward, right and left until loosing orientation completely. You know by entering a maze that there is an escape and you seek desperately for the exit. That's the dangerous moment when you might grab any saving straw, respond to other's advice and opinion. As the maze in our lives isn't something external, as it represents your inner world only you are able to know the way out! You need the help of a person who doesn't paint her colors on your life canvas. You need the assistance of a neutral expert, as desperate times call for extraordinary measures.

Hitch your love to a star

Do you know that you already hitched your love to a star? This book you are reading right now is that star. It acts like a mentor and is at your side whenever you want. The website ButterflyHabits.com is designed for your needs only. It's the place to go when you seek assistance and help. On my blog you will always find more secrets and smart strategies to keep yourself empowered, inspired and motivated. All tools, resources, services and programs offered are designed to guide you to happiness and fulfillment in love. Stay in touch, and benefit. Get the knowledge and wisdom on how to remove the thorns of love.

Having a Coach represents the ultimate opportunity for unleashing your woman's power to claim and aim the relationship you want. Let's have a look about the difference between mentoring and coaching that a relationship expert may offer. While my Mentoring programs train skills and behavior, Coaching is a more customized assistance.

Today countless institutes and schools are offering coach trainings. No wonder that people are confused about all the different certificates. There are Coaches with a certification done in just one weekend or during a week. And others with years of learning, training and experience. As your love is a most important treasure, you want to make sure you have an ethical and experienced coach at your side. So, what are the crucial considerations when deciding on a personal, high-level trained relationship coach?

NoGo #1

A professional coach doesn't apply advices or solutions

An expert coach remains in a state of neutrality and doesn't mix personal life experiences with yours. Therefore professional coaches avoid offering personal advices or solutions, instead causing change by connecting you to your inner source of wisdom and guidance.

NoGo #2

A professional coach avoids "closed questions"

Closed questions are those which offer you only the option to answer with Yes or No. Those kinds of questions are undesirable in the professional coaching world, as they neither inspire nor stimulate your mind. A professional expert coach will apply high-quality, open-ended question techniques to leverage your insights, and make you determine your "blind spots."

NoGo #3

A professional coach never makes you dependent

One of the highest, ethical principles of a professional coaching practice is to make you find the solution, and reach the target on your own. The ultimate goal of coaching is to strengthen the self-confidence of the coachee. That's why a professional coach is not allowed to lead you on a journey you can't handle yourself. Also, this principle is valid when approaching a delicate topic during a session. A professional coach will always ask you if deeper exploration is desired before going ahead with further questions.

The final question … is all about trust

When you enjoyed your first coaching session and evaluated a qualified professional coach you still need to find an answer on one question:

Do you trust this coach?

This question stands outside of the terms of professionalism. Trust is the core bond to your coach. When you don't experience an ongoing sense of trust, I strongly recommend that you check out other coaches. As you are going to work on intimate topics, it is absolutely essential to have a solid relationship based upon trust with your coach. A trusted coach will support your courage and self-confidence as you confront the challenges.

Get more information about coaching on FannyRitter.com.

Challenge your needs for a coach

- In what aspects of your life do you seek assistance that would generate more harmony in your relationship?
- If you won't ask for help, what may be the worst-case scenario?
- What would be the likelihood in percentage that this worst-case will happen?
- If you would ask for help, what may be the worst that could happen?
- If you would seek out and accept assistance, how will your life and relationship become enhanced?

Chapter 14

Insights of the world's
most ambitious women

If you were born without wings,
do nothing to prevent them from growing.

∽ Coco Chanel

You are about to conclude your journey through this book. Now, you own expert knowledge to claim and attain a fulfilling relationship, how to rekindle the sparks in togetherness, master challenges and rely on your inner power and strength. From this moment, you know how to get what you want in love. Sure, this book offers a huge "pie" of Butterfly Habits and you may feel overwhelmed. Like at the beginning of the book I remind you not to eat the pie in one entire piece. Do some cherry picking. Take your time to train and make a specific habit grow. Don't wake up your amygdala! Be compassionate with yourself during your endeavor to love. The moment will come when your abilities turn into an automatic reflex, a Butterfly Habit. And by the way: remind yourself to honor and celebrate every tiny, single achievement. The reward of your daily persistence is having developed a solid happiness from inside out that will allow you to enjoy your love for a lifetime.

Get inspired!

To make this book even more valuable, I am happy to offer you insights from some of the world's most ambitious women. Enjoy these unique insights, as these interviews are only published in this book. Let yourself be touched by the hearts and minds of extraordinary women of our time.

Irina, Countess of Plettenberg-Lenhausen

Irina's amazing career mirrors her unique leadership talent and lists numerous Fortune 500 corporations. 1990, KOMMERSANT the largest business newspaper in Russia, elected her the "Business Lady of the Year." Although not a Russian, she received this honor because of her mediation deal of the largest single business in Russia for NCR—with the first of three payments of USD 1.5 billion. Irina is an inspiring, fascinating person whose natural warmth holds peoples' attention. She is an amazing example of the beauty in maintaining balance between professional success and fulfillment in love.

Interview with Irina, Countess of Plettenberg-Lenhausen

In your opinion, what is the biggest challenge in a relationship between man and woman?

The biggest challenge is to understand each other. Without understanding, everything else is merely an "intent." I think if there is understanding, all other steps are easier, more elegant and will bring people closer to each other. I think that's the foundation of a relationship.

"Understanding" refers here to the inner comprehension or the verbal, outside understanding?

Understanding means when people understand each other without words. Not only in a discussion or exchange, but when there exists an understanding about establishing a relationship. When you really take note of what the partner thinks, how he "ticks" and how you are able to live together as a couple.

Which are your personal secrets or strategies to meet this challenge?

I don't know if I have a secret. I always try to listen first and then speak. I think in many relationships, the couple believes that they are sharing deeply when they are only talking superficially or not actually listening to the other. I am very attentive in this respect. I'm trying to understand what my partner wants me to hear. My response and reaction come afterwards. I think this is crucial. But the most important thing is love. When he is really "your" person then even the most difficult situation and greatest challenge will lead to a good end. I believe:

Love is everything and love is a beginning.

Not only in your relationship but also in your work, leisure, family, environment and nature. Love represents the absolute foundation for everything.

What influence has the self-esteem of a woman on her relationship? What opportunities and potential risks arise?

Self-esteem is extremely important. Only when a woman possesses self-esteem is she able to communicate with her partner on the same level. This makes relationship's life much easier. If a woman feels suppressed due to a lack of self-confidence, I think this relationship will fail. Maybe not immediately, but over time.

In the fairytale of the frog prince, the frog transforms into a prince by a kiss. Referring to this, what are your thoughts about its impact on the relationship between man and woman?

Every fairytale owns significant core wisdom. In this case it's: "Back to Love." If you offer a man love, warmth, closeness, or—as in the story—a kiss, then he gets stimulated to become better. It's like praising. My husband is a world champion in praising. It has always the effect of an incentive for me. If I'm praised or kissed, I think: "You grow into something more beautiful, you grow into something greater." It encourages me to be better, to do better. A frog into a prince: by a kiss? I strongly believe in it! I am convinced that we should embrace and kiss each other as much as possible. Maybe, even one time too much than one time too few. Because we don't know how many times are left. Do it today, now, in the moment rather than later only to discover that later never arrived. Therefore, kiss each frog into a prince!

Studies show: if a woman's work hours increase also the risk of divorce increases, while an increase in the working hours of the man mostly demonstrates no statistical impact on the divorce rate. What are, in your opinion, the three factors to be successful in both career and personal partnership?

I think this also requires a lot of understanding. All marriages and couples are unique and consist of two distinct individuals. There is no recipe for a perfect relationship. Not even for a perfect gazpacho, as each wife prepares them after its own: a bit more salt, pepper, a few herbs. The same happens to relationships. There are women who master working more hours, while still making their husbands and families happy. And there are women who don't work yet their families are unhappy. The only recipe I know is as follows: "Look inside yourself and find your own recipe deeply hidden in your heart, for you and your loved ones. You are unique. You don't fit into a frame."

Studies also show that challenges in communication are one of the top factors for an impending divorce. What are your personal strategies to master successfully communication challenges in your relationship?

I think the best strategy is to listen, let the other speak and remain calm. Saying to yourself as a Coach: "I will stay calm, regardless of whether a confrontation emerges of we engage in healthy discussion. I will take note of everything

internally as peaceful as possible and won't respond immediately. I'll take a break and will ask myself the question:
"Why did I let it get so far that this discussion got possible?" In case of a divorce, marriage, love and kiss there
are always two parties. Why should only one be guilty in a
dispute? When you first have a look at what you've done
wrong getting this far, then there would always be found a
compromise in a dispute or conflict. Because the one who
masters the art of compromise will be master of the relationship! I think you should not try to change your partner.
You should change yourself. As an example, the weather
can't be changed . . . but you find the right clothes. The
same way you should consider another person, your partner,
beloved ones, friends and family. You just need to find the
right clothes. As an Norwegian saying goes: There is no bad
weather; there is only inappropriate clothing.

*What is your personal secret to a successful and fulfilling
relationship?*

Love. Love in every situation: even if you're angry. The
moment you're upset, remember you that you love this man
and can forgive everything. To forgive is a greater happiness
as any gift or beautiful, common hour. When you consider how generous you are in this moment. If you forgive
the other, you understand him deeply and love him more
than anything. See this as an opportunity to demonstrate
your love. I am convinced that you will be rewarded only
positively.

*Irina, if you could give a woman a final relationship advice:
what would it be, what would you tell her?*

Find the right one. Don't stay where you feel discomfort. Shouldn't he have your second heart? If he doesn't, then be tough enough to end the relationship conciliatory and friendly. Stop or plan a relationship break! Find your second heart, and don't continue to live in captivity.

Why man has two eyes, two ears, two hands, two feet,
but only one heart? I think we all have two hearts,
but we have to find our second heart.
And we have a lifetime opportunity.
When a person in our lives decides to leave us,
I personally won't try to hold him back.
Because a person with our second heart would
remain with us, regardless of when we find him,
whether we are 18 or 58 years old.

∿ Irina, Countess of Plettenberg-Lenhausen

Tori (Victoria) Murden McClure

is an explorer and fascinating personality. She is the first woman to ski the geographic South Pole and she is also the first woman to make a solo crossing of the Atlantic Ocean by rowboat. Her book, *A Pearl in the Storm*, captivates the reader with a passionate heroine's journey and an open hearted story of romance with her husband, Mac.

Tori has served as a chaplain, an executive director of a shelter for homeless women, a public policy analyst for the Mayor of Louisville, and she worked for the boxer and humanitarian Muhammad Ali. In 2010, she was named president of Spalding University in Louisville, Kentucky. She served as Chair of the Board of the National Outdoor Leadership School until June 2012.

Interview with Tori Murden McClure

Tori, in a speech you wrote for the mayor of Louisville you used the following sentence: "A rainbow of excellence that lights the cosmic dark."

In your opinion, what are the components of a rainbow of excellence that light a relationship?

Trust is one of the elements that lights a relationship . . . that you can tell your partner anything . . . that it will be taken in and absorbed and considered. Then I think fun is really an important component . . . to enjoy one another's company, as we too often take ourselves far too seriously. And love, obviously, is a significant component.

Before you started writing your book A Pearl in the Storm, *Thor Heyerdahl suggested: "Be sure to leave room enough to grow." How does this advice show relevance in a personal relationship?*

Certainly in the United States I see the tendency of folks to get into a relationship thinking they are going to change or alter their partner, make him do the growing. I think that is very wrong-headed; we must grow together. Everyone needs to recognize that leaving room for one another to grow, to change and develop new ideas and points of view is really important.

Here, at the university, I had a difficult last year. A member of the board was making my life really difficult. I was challenged in a way I was unaccustomed to being challenged. And to be able to go home to Mac and have him just be there for me in a solid way was so important to keeping my sense of identity, my sense of security, my sense of leadership . . . and to be able to go back to the institution and not let this one person upset my balance.

> The greatest freedom allotted to any human
> is the freedom to choose one's attitude.
> Whatever the weather, it is my weather,
> and I must do my best to enjoy it.
>
> ～ Tori Murden McClure, *A Pearl in the Storm*

Relationships can suddenly experience a "climate" change. From your perspective, Tori, which is the most powerful attitude to face an "area of low pressure" in a relationship?
I think hope is really important. There are storms and tumults in any relationship. But there will come another day; there will come a change of weather. You just can't run away when things get tough. And there is that notion of the most powerful thing we have is the ability to chose one's attitude. Victor Frankl's *Man's Search for Meaning* is the influence for that opinion in my own mind. Victor Frankl lived through a concentration camp and he kept in mind the image of his beloved, of his wife. And Frankl thought that image of someone whom he loved more than anything was what kept him alive. In those storms to remember what's good about the relationship, to remember why you fell in love with this person is very important. Because sometimes, when things are really tough, we are not nice, we are not lovable, we are not kind. And to be able to remember the hope of a brighter day is truly essential.

Somewhere in the silence of the sea I learned to listen.

∽ Tori Murden McClure, A *Pearl in the Storm*

What should a woman listen to in her relationship, Tori?

I am an introvert and quiet person. I would say, before my row across the ocean, I didn't trust my feminine side. I didn't trust my instincts and I didn't trust my emotions. And listening to yourself, trusting yourself in a way that leaves space for another is important. Being secure in yourself . . . in some way self-sufficient . . . but knowing where your empty places are. Recognizing that, in my case the man I love, fills up those places where I don't feel secure and I don't feel strong. The willingness to be quiet and be at peace, not necessarily listening to the words but to the underlying music is important.

Tori, in your book you wrote ". . . with problems there are no right answers, only right reactions." In a relationship: what distinguishes a right reaction or a wrong reaction?

There is a tendency—particularly with men—they want to solve the problem. And going back to the example of the board member who made my life miserable, my husband wanted to solve the problem. But I didn't need him to fix the problem as much as I needed him to understand my misery, and be with me in that misery. And I needed him just to be supportive, caring and loving . . . because the problem isn't necessarily something that has an easy solution. I am a classic problem solver and I love puzzles. But so often we jump ahead trying to solve the problem, while the folks who are in the storm need me to say, "I care, I love you, I am here for you, it's going to take a lot to solve this problem and I will be with you through the storm."

I remember when I was working as a hospital chaplain a wise adviser said to me "Don't just do something, sit there!" (She laughs) And now I understand the meaning. Sometimes the doing gets in the way of the being.

Your friend Joseph Curran once said: "You can't travel the road of wisdom in a feather bed." Is this also true when a woman is looking for wisdom to master her relationship?

I think the strength of a relationship is built on a rocky road. On the other hand, we don't have to make things difficult to have a good relationship. My husband Mac is really wonderful, I am tremendously lucky and our relationship is a featherbed most days. I don't think that we have to go looking for troubles, but I know that I learn more from the storms than I do from the calm seas.

"Men need to be needed even more than they need to be loved . . . ," which is also a quote from your book. How should a woman keep your quote in mind regarding her relationship?

As I consider myself a strong and independent woman, sometimes I forget that Mac needs me to need him. And at times he prefers the storm, because in the storm I shall come home to him and look for his counsel and look for his care and love. When things are sunny and bright then I don't need him as much and he might wonder whether I love him . . . and I absolutely do . . . but he doesn't have that constant reminder that I depend upon him.

Where men tend to be defined by their actions,
women tend to be defined by their relationships.

↪ Tori Murden McClure, *A Pearl in the Storm*

*For a woman: what kind of dangers or limitations might arise
from that statement?*

We sometimes get limited. The only stories women are
allowed to tell about themselves are mostly relationship
driven. The typical hero's story is the journey of a man,
almost always a white man who has money or is on his way
to getting some money. And the women's story is the fall-in-
love romance. *A Pearl in the Storm* is a hero's story, hero's
story, hero's story—romance! And for me, the treasure of
the end of my hero's journey was the fall-in-love. And when
my book was published, first I thought, "Oh no—I sold out!
I was going to write the hero's journey for women . . . I sold
out . . . I turned it into a romance . . . how could I have
done that!" And then I watched videos of myself getting
out of the rowboat by literally stepping into Mac's arms.
And all sorts of pictures taken around that time I describe
as: "they were pathetic!" (She laughs) I was so in love that
I couldn't wait to get back to him. It was, what it was. The
hero's journey is a story of action, and romance is a story
of relationship. I think we have to give men space to have
their romantic story and we need to get women space to
have their hero's story—for the quest.

It is my opinion that big mistakes don't kill people
in the wilderness, little mistakes do.

↪ Tori Murden McClure, *A Pearl in the Storm*

What are little mistakes that might kill a relationship?

I have never thought about that in terms of relationships, but it's a wonderful point. When I think about friends who have gotten in really bad situations, it was not because they were bad climbers or bad mountaineers—they were bad campers. They didn't take enough food and they didn't stay warm. I think this question is a wonderful point for relationships because it's not the big mistakes that ruin a relationship; it's the small, day-to-day, inattentive insults. It's the little thing that we don't attend to that kills a partnership, not the big thing. We tend to overlook that monumental mistake, when we think it's a one-time mistake . . . but instead . . . we should count the mistakes that happen every day. I think it's very true that the little things make or break a relationship.

My favorite moment in the day is when I turn my car home toward Mac.

> I intended to slay the sea monster of my
> helplessness. but I am a woman. We don't slay
> our dragons; we embrace them.
>
> ✑ Tori Murden McClure, *A Pearl in the Storm*

If women would embrace their "weakness," how could this enhance their relationships?

I have learned . . . as a leader, and particularly as female leader, that always being strong, always having the answers, always being in a position that says "I am right" actually diminishes my leadership . . . that I am better off when I am uncertain about things: "I don't know which way to go."

And, that vulnerability, that sense of openness, that sense of questioning gives the people around me an opportunity to exercise their leadership and bring forward the good ideas. In a relationship, it's important to be vulnerable, to be open, to be soft—and I am not at all a soft woman (she laughs)—to be comfortable with uncertainty. Over time in a relationship we learn a tolerance with adversity, and we learn a certain comfort with uncertainty. These are important qualities. The thing I see is that folks haven't developed enough self-awareness to be ready to enter into a relationship. If you don't know who you are alone . . . how can you figure out who you are in a partnership? So many young peoples are diving too quickly into relationships that are not right for them.

If you could offer one final advice to a woman in a relationship: what would it be?
    Have fun! When I think of Mac: he brightens my day, he makes me smile and we have a lot of fun together.

> One of the best things about having taken
> a rowboat alone across the atlantic ocean
> is that now as a leader, I feel comfortable.
> if I feel like crying, I cry, and no one thinks
> that I am weak.

> ✎ Tori Murden McClure

Holly Carinci

Holly became a publicist because she needed one and there weren't any that met her criteria, so she "switched hats." She grew her company HollyWords Publicity into a very successful business, worked for dozens of famous actors, directors and producers. Also, Holly is the founder and CEO of the Canadian Awards for Electronic and Animated Arts (CAEAA). The show, later known as the ELAN Awards, had a successful 3-year run in Vancouver for which Holly landed as Host celebrities William Shatner, Seth MacFarlane (Family Guy) and Tom Kenny (Sponge-Bob Square Pants©). Holly is an extraordinary woman, professionally and personally, and her wonderful laughter is so charming and enchanting—you cannot resist.

Interview with Holly Carinci

Holly, in your opinion: What is today's biggest challenge in a relationship between man and woman?

Roles. That would be my one-word answer. Women's roles in their professional lives have progressed but not in their personal lives. I believe that we don't know what our roles are and men don't know what their roles are. Neither knows what they're supposed to do in a relationship any more. As women, we are empowered in our professional lives and the importance of our roles has just skyrocketed. Women are almost running the world now.

But when we are in a relationship with a man, we are not sure any more who's supposed to take out the garbage, who's supposed to do the laundry or whatever the case may be. It makes us insecure. When we are in our jobs we know exactly what we are supposed to do. As an example, I am the VP Marketing; say that's my job title. With our significant other we don't know what our job title is any more. We don't know how to manage it.

What is the biggest error/fault a woman should avoid doing in her relationship?

Not allowing him to help. We need to accept his help and start saying yes. And again we go back to roles. Personally, I have a very feminine side, but going through life I used my male energy as my source of power. When I changed it back to female it worked wonderfully for me and was so much easier.

As women, we have come to the point that we don't need a lot of help and can do almost anything ourselves . . . that is admirable. Therefore we often say: "Thank you, honey, I appreciate it, but I've got it."

That's not correct. I think that we really need to say: "Oh, thank you, I need that help." I think in a relationship we need to be a lot more open to the man in our life, to accept his assistance. Men want to be our heroes—that's their nature, for most of them. They want to help us. That doesn't mean that we are helpless, or anything like that—it's a fine balance. Let them help. It will make a world of difference.

Studies reveal that a lack of preparation for marriage is indicated as one of the top reasons for relationship's failure. Let's assume you would found a school to close this gap: Which school subjects would you teach and why?

There's actually only one that comes to mind and it is really important: Communications. The ability to listen to each other is enormous, just enormous. To really hear what each is saying. That summarizes all. I can't think of other courses, because every relationship is different and has its own dynamic. I think when you have great communication then it brings on appreciation; you're hearing each other, what you want, your needs, etc.—you're set.

What could men learn from women and vice versa?

My immediate answer to the first half of the question is too long and the answer to the second half of the question is too short. (She laughs.) That doesn't mean that I don't appreciate men. In fact, I love men! I just think that even the smartest man in the world is quite simple. So let's leave it with that before I get myself in too much hot water

I am a leader and a team player; I am broadly creative and finely focused; I am passionate and compassionate.

⌒ Holly Carinci

Thinking a moment about those rich, professional qualities, Holly: What, in your opinion, inhibits many women to implement their professional skills in their personal lives and relationships?

We gain confidence and security in ourselves a lot more easily in our professional lives with a greater support system. When we do well, we are told that we do well—for the most part. We know our subjects, we know our roles and we go and perform them. We have people giving us accolades all the time; we get promotions and new job titles, raises in our pay, etc. We are knowledgeable in what we do and confident in our abilities to do it.

Conversely, in our personal relationships we do not have that comfort zone or that confidence. We can easily handle a critique in a boardroom, and manage it quite easily, and defuse it. Whereby a comment from our significant other about the suit we are wearing as we walk out the door can ruin our entire day. We need to find that balance. We need to take that home with us.

Reading your following quote . . .

"I have landed feature cover stories for my clients; I myself have been featured in cover stories." I was wondering: in which way might self-promotion and branding skills help a woman in her personal relationship? What could be some first steps to activate those skills?

That's a great question. Let's say that you go into a new relationship, or you're just meeting a new person whom you find interesting, and you take those self-promotion, or "branding skills," in with you at the beginning. That's the scenario I see. I think it is fantastic. In a relationship, saying the words like I said in my quote, not in a humble way and not coming off as a braggart . . . just truthful. I think that the man in a woman's life needs to be able to handle that power. Needs to understand who she is. Because: that is who she is. That is her professional life . . . a good half of her. She needs to let him know that. And the "right" man admires that and supports it and is proud of her . . . and that's big . . . "proud of her" . . . not intimidated, but proud . . . and stands behind her. Most men in relationships feel intimidated by women's power today, but that's too big of a subject to go into here. . . . Let's talk about that in your second book! A woman doesn't have to down-play what she does. The men who can't handle that—dismiss her achievements or make light of them—right off the top: you've got to take them to the trash. By branding and promotion off the top you will pretty much find out who passes the test. Don't take time and don't wait to do it to "feel him out" and see if it's "safe." Do it off the top by saying clearly: "This is who I am professionally." Any man who down-plays that . . . forget about . . . to the trash. Come from who you are.

Holly, your next quote refers to your professional work:
"If you would like to have that power placed behind your endeavour . . ." What kind of power may favor a woman's endeavour of a personal relationship? How can a woman get access to that power and make it grow?

I think that power in the relationship for a woman is a deep feeling of peace with herself. It's right from the belly, heart, soul and mind. She knows herself and is really at peace and happy and open to everything around her. Be it professionally, as a housewife, as a mother, as a sister, as a wife . . . all of her roles in her life she is at peace and happy with . . . that is a remarkable power to bring into a relationship. Because that woman will really be open to everything that's happening, be willing to change, be interested, and be listening . . . that is the biggest power.

> The difference between ordinary
> and extraordinary is that little extra.
>
> ⌐ Jimmy Johnson

Referring to that quote: What makes a relationship EXTRA-ordinary?

It's that little extra-thing you do . . . whether you know that he plans to get up and be ready before you and to head out of the door to that big meeting . . . and he doesn't have to worry about making the coffee . . . no matter how big your day is, you have gotten up and done something very small and special.

That makes a relationship extraordinary and there could be a million examples like that. I think when you put yourself aside, just a little bit—sure, you could use that extra sleep—but you get up and make sure that this is really a big day for him . . . that's just one example that makes a relationship extraordinary.

If you could offer one final advice to a woman in a relationship: what would it be?

To make sure that the person that you are with knows you and supports you . . . completely. Only then, from that place of knowing, can a sustaining love for one-another grow.

Doris Hefti

Can you imagine an encounter on a park bench as the starting point of an amazing career?

Being a young, simple country girl with braids, as Doris Hefti describes herself, she was in San Remo, Italy, sitting on a bench and observing the sophisticated atmosphere of the town. An elegant, American lady sat down beside the young girl and fate took its course. For many years, Estée Lauder personally mentored the country girl who grew up and had an outstanding career. In the year 2007, Doris Hefti's exceptional achievements were honored as she received the "Estée Lauder Brand Manager of the Year" for having promoted the brand from zero to a multimillion-dollar business in Switzerland.

Interview with Doris Hefti

Life is about not knowing, having to change,
taking the moment and making the best of it,
without knowing what's going to happen next.

⌐ Gilda Radner, comedian and actress

Many years ago, because you met by chance Estée Lauder in San Remo, Italy and she became your mentor, this quote has come true and launched your career. This quote is also valid for the relationship of couples. In your opinion: Today, what is the biggest challenge in a relationship between man and woman?

The zeitgeist is changing. Forty years ago, women were different than today. The challenge arises when a couple does not live the same zeitgeist. When I first met my husband, we were like two identical, polished dice. We came together and worked together. In personal life the aspect of man/woman comes into play and there exist different standards in this regard today.

The single most important career decision
that a woman makes is whether she will have a
life partner and who that partner is.

⌐ Sheryl Sandberg, Lean in

Regarding this quote: What should a woman consider when making this decision? What questions should she ask herself?

The biggest challenge is to find the man with the characteristics you desire and to possess within oneself the

191

matching characteristics if your intent is marriage. A woman who has a professional career and plans to preserve this path must also know when to enter into a relationship. A critical question the woman has to ask herself especially if she intends to maintain a career: is this man reliable? The question about the personal level of the relationship between "man/woman" then still isn't answered. You have to distinguish those two things. I think we have to act differently in the future and have to learn how to keep separate business life and private life.

What impact has the woman's self-image on her relationship? What opportunities and potential risks open up?

If I had not had the good fortune to meet Estée Lauder and to learn from all that I did about growing a business and having an impact throughout the world, then my husband would have dominated our relationship. I have learned so much from her. Charisma is important. Movements, gestures, body language in general are signals women need to notice and understand. Many women are not aware of this. The more you know what you can about your partner, the better you can assert yourself. However, you should be honest with yourself. In case you only lead to believe instead of really master things, you should learn doing them. Men will notice that. In this aspect men tend to be very sensitive. In knowledge, decisions, actions . . . men have a sixth sense. Whatever may happen, the goal is important. A woman who has significant achievements in her career commands the respect of her husband, especially if she attains results and success, which he himself hasn't attained.

Setting basic rules and principles from the beginning of a relationship: What do you think of it? What should be considered in particular?

I am also of this opinion—that one should set basic rules and principles. Yes, absolutely! However, one must be careful not to be too zealous in the effort. Approach the adventure of identifying rules and principles for life and relationships slowly, deliberately. Otherwise, you might wind up scaring away your man!

In a newspaper interview, you mentioned that during meetings you had your child with you. You succeeded in balancing your outstanding career with being a mother. What challenges did you face as a working mother in your relationship? How did you master them?

We started "Estée Lauder Switzerland" from zero. No business, no employees, no budget. I was alone. So I began to organize beauty teas to present the Estée Lauder products. I put my child in a wicker basket, lined with soft blankets, and placed the basket on a cloth on the floor beneath the table. I then focused on the women, encouraging them to seek and enhance their own beauty. At this time my husband was responsible for the distributors while I took care of the sale. My child was part of all. She never interfered: neither in our business nor our relationship. She was just always with us.

The real question young women would like to ask
superstars like Sheryl Sandberg and Anne Marie Slaughter
is not just
"How do you succeed professionally?" but also,
"How do you build a personal life
that supports your career?"
I'd like to see a leadership training program that guides
and supports young women in doing precisely that.[21]

⌐ Leslie C. Bell, Ph.D.

What kind of thoughts generates this statement?

Today it is different: the young generation possesses a greater sense of self-confidence. They also demonstrate so much more trust in the future. In contrast, I approached everything very seriously and fearfully . . . that's what I was taught. Years ago, you used to have anxiety when you did not achieve your goals. Be it business, school grades, and sales. All that generated anxiety. Today this has changed. I have often to deal with young bankers. They say: I'm working on my career until I'm 28 years old. Then I can get married and will have an understanding of a relationship. This is very different from my generation. Young people approach a relation-ship differently. This generation sees marriage as much more valuable, on a completely different basis. In my view, the reason lies mainly in the course of education. Today, mothers raise their children in another way.

Leadership in the context of that quote refers to the personal character, which can't be bought. A woman can just learn it. This requires practice. Only when you prove char-acter in the practical application, you will own leadership.

Everything that crowns professional success brings assistance to personal relationship's life. Every man takes a bow, the more success you prove. The higher your success, the deeper his bow.

Finally, if you could give women advice for her relationship: what would it be? What would you tell her?
Unfortunately, many women who are married to good partners don't appreciate their partner, don't work at making the relationship stronger, instead they just focus on having a good time. A man requires more than having a good time. I suggest women acquire a good education, to be proficient both in business and in finance, to learn languages, to be efficient instead of just busy. This means demonstrating results. It is important to be honest and not deceive yourself. This is the starting point for requests in any relationship.

Everything that crowns professional success
brings assistance to personal relationship's life.
Every man takes a bow, the more success you prove.
The higher your success, the deeper his bow.

∽ Doris Hefti

Rosie Meleady

In her 20s, Rosie created a multi-million dollar non-profit magazine, which gave instant financial support to the homeless and long-term unemployed. For starting the magazine, she received the gold "President's Award" from the Irish President Mary Robinson. At 24 years old, Rosie became the youngest woman to receive the prestigious "International Women in Publishing New Venture Award." Rosie is a passionate entrepreneur who now runs a wedding planning business and the Magazine Creation Academy, which teaches people how to start their own online magazine to share their passions with the world while creating an income.

Interview with Rosie Meleady

In your opinion, Rosie: What is today's biggest challenge in a relationship between man and woman?

The biggest challenge is that people have an image of what a perfect relationship and partner should be. Living the images of perfection from movies, TVs, media and thinking that everybody else has a perfect life—not knowing what is happening behind the closed doors. Don't compare yourself to other people. When the honeymoon phase is over, everybody faces some challenges, and if you get through those challenges together, you are helping each other to grow. It's actually a partnership of self-development. In a relationship, one can't grow in each other's shadow—you have to give space to each other to grow together. It is a lot easier for people to step away from a challenging situation. You see this with celebrities all the time. If you face up to things and get through together, your relationship will be stronger as a result of that. I think the challenge couples have today is their image of perfection: their image how a relationship should be and how to move through something together.

You created a non-profit-magazine to support homeless and long-term unemployed. Your passion to help and to enhance others' lives highly impressed me. How can a woman integrate that quality in her relationship and—at the same time—ensure to stay connected with her personal dreams and needs—not losing herself for other's well-being?

A lot of women are passionate about helping others. When I was young I went on protest marches to free Nelson Mandela, joined Greenpeace and did all that sort of stuff as I wanted to change the world!

My husband and I had the same vision of starting a street magazine in Ireland and that's how we met; we went on to set up the magazine together. When we had our first child we realized that we had to step back. We asked ourselves: what are our goals? What do we want for our children?

You have to set your priorities. Don't neglect whom you love while helping others! You need to take time for yourself and your partner. I see so many people living up to their career, living up to that what they think is expected from them: to be the perfect wife, the perfect mother, the perfect partner and a perfect businesswoman. You can't do everything! Something has to give. And women often feel they have to climb to the top of the ladder to prove themselves. But then, when they have children and they are dropping them off at childcare for 12-hour days, they are torn between wanting to be with their kids more and living up to the career expectation of getting promoted. In a partnership you have to decide what both of you want, what your goals are, agree about them and then work towards them. If one of your goals is helping other people: brilliant, do it! But don't feel you have to do everything.

You were honored with the gold "President Award" for your street magazine project. Rosie, what do you think about the importance of recognition in a personal relationship? What "awards" or "ceremonies" could offer a woman to the significant one in her life?

In relationship start up years, a lot of people feel gifts are important: the most expensive engagement ring, the biggest diamond. But as you get into a relationship, small things matter more. Offering support and encouragement when your partner needs it, is much better than buying fancy gifts. Little things count. For example I prefer the fact that my husband brings me breakfast in bed on a Sunday morning rather than a bunch of flowers!

Besides financial support, your magazine showed people how to make a difference in the world by small actions. How may small actions make a difference in a relationship?

Getting to know when to talk and when to stay quiet . . . at the right time . . . is important as well. (She laughs). And that is a very small action. It's hard to learn but once you know that technique it is very effective. (She laughs again).

Offering assistance to others is a wonderful attribute, be it in professional or personal life. In your opinion, Rosie: How important is it to maintain a balance between giving and receiving in a relationship? How can a woman cultivate it?

Good question. When we look at movies and TV and see "perfect balance," the man is doing the washing up or the woman is divorcing because he is not washing up. (She laughs). It is to drop the perception of what is expected and live your life rather than the life of other people. You have to give and not expect to receive. Giving yourself and everything you have and not expecting to get it back. There will always be an imbalance but over the years it evens out. Sometimes, in my relationship I needed a lot of support, a lot of encouragement, and my husband was there for me. And I was there for him at bad times. It has balanced out over the years. So you just have to give and you will receive back. *Also, you are the editor of* Life Is Short, *a free, online, inspirational magazine. Your magazine's title triggered my following question. Living that slogan* Life Is Short *in a personal relationship: how could that enhance a personal relationship?*

If you are living together, little things could really grow to resentments. In my partnership, we have learned to give and to take. Don't get obsessed with the small things and look at the bigger picture: that you have found love and that you respect each other. And also to laugh easily . . . it's so important that you laugh and smile in a relationship every day, to appreciate little things and not to focus on the negative. Forget the small stuff and look at the bigger picture!

Life Is Short *magazine shows people how you can follow a life of passion. Rosie, what is your personal secret to create a relationship of passion?*

When there are storms in your relationship don't get freaked about things you can't control. Once you get through some major things, your relationship gets stronger. You learn and grow as a person, you both will learn in your relationship. You will appreciate each other for doing that. And as you develop as a person you get to know what is acceptable and what is not acceptable in your life, relationships and business. You become a stronger and wiser person.

You directed a promotional campaign called "The Ultimate Job in the World." How can a relationship become "The Ultimate Job in the World?"

A relationship is the biggest job in the world! It takes a lot of work and is a lifelong project that you commit to. But if you are willing to put the work into, you will develop as a better person as the relationship develops. The ultimate job and goal is actually to succeed and to say: "We did it!"

Rosie, we both are born under the astrological sign of Pisces— known as compassionate individuals and harmony seekers. Which strengthening and "weakening" effects might arise from two different "characters" in a relationship? And how could challenges be overcome?

Sometimes you don't always like the same things. Travel, for example, was a huge part of my life, but my husband is afraid of flying. That was a big obstacle. I like adventure style vacations. So I went on a few with a friend rather than with my husband. It was fantastic because it gave me "me time," time to be by myself, and be me.

Sometimes you can lose yourself in a relationship, especially when there are children involved. You can actually forget who you are, helping everybody else. Sometimes you need to get back to being you and what you love to do. And those trips were my opportunity to step away and get back in touch with who I am. Without taking anybody else into consideration for 10 days I could do what I wanted to do. It was a fabulous experience. I call them my "me-time trips."

Sometimes it needs some push to do that and get back into what you love to do—because your confidence has gone a little bit. But it's a good thing to do as you get back to being the person your partner originally fell in love with so when you return they love you all the more! I encourage people to do what they love to do, and not always to include their partner. Now my husband loves travelling as we bought a campervan so we don't have to fly!

If you could offer one final piece of advice to a woman in a relationship: what would it be?

Make sure that there is give-and-take . . . and that you laugh easily. When somebody makes you laugh, smile and happy, you've struck gold! Don't sweat the small stuff and look at the bigger picture! Look at what you have found in your partner. Focus on that rather than on what irritates you about them!

In a partnership you have to decide what both of you want,
what your goals are, agree about them and
then work towards them.

༄ Rosie Meleady

Chapter 15

Au revoir

Your journey to a fulfilled relationship doesn't end here. The truth is: it has just begun. I firmly believe that mastering relationships is the only real achievement in life. Whether that relationship is with your partner, family, children, friends, colleagues or strangers—all you want in life is available through mastering relationship. Challenge your creativity and get rid of dark "clouds" in your partnership. Brighten your love's sky! Enjoy the wonderful, emerging feeling of being your man's number one. As a final Butterfly Habit, I want you to look up to the sky at night and watch for the stars. You are like them: brilliant and awesome in the universe of love and life. I am with you, wherever you are—in heart and mind.

Au revoir doesn't mean good-bye, it means "Until we see you again."

Notes:

1. Edward N. Lorenz. Professor of Meteorology. Predictability: Does the flap of a butterfly's wing in Brazil set off a tornado in Texas? *American Association for the Advancement of Science*: 1972.

2. Robert Maurer. *One Small Step Can Change Your Life: The Kaizen Way*. Workman Publishing. New York: 2004.

3. The National Marriage Project. The State of Our Unions: Marriage in America 2011: How Parenthood Makes Life Meaningful and How Marriage Makes Parenthood Bearable. stateofourunions. org. [Accessed: April 28, 2013]

4. *Huffington Post*. "Census: Divorces decline in United States." May 18, 2011. huffingtonpost.com/2011/05/18/census-divorces-decline-i_n_863639.html. [Accessed: May 13, 2013.]

5. facts.randomhistory.com/divorce-facts.html. [Accessed: May 13, 2013.]

6. John H. Johnson. 2004. Examined data from the Survey of Income and Program Participation.

7. Louis Harris Survey. http://dailyemerald.com/2006/02/08/the-world-of-academia-after-the-wordsi-do. [Accessed: May 20, 2013.]

8. Jose Olalla. Our unique observer in the world. Annual Conference of the International Coach Federation (ICF): 2007.

9. Noel Burch. *Four Stages for Learning Any New Skill*. Gordon Training International: 1970s.

10. John Meyer; Natalie Allen. Three Component Model of Commitment. *Human Resource Management Review*: 1991.

11. Alan J. Hawkins; Tamara A. Fackrell. Should I keep Trying to Work it Out? Chapter 3 by William H. Doherty: How common is divorce and what are the reasons? Reference note "With this ring . . . A national survey on marriage in America. (2005). Gaithersburg, MD: The National Fatherhood Initiative." *Utah Commission on Marriage*: 2009.

12. Boglarka Hadinger. Armes Opfer oder faszinierende Frau? (Poor victim or fascinating woman?) "Fragen unseres Daseins"—ORF-Funkhaus. Dornbirn: 2006.

13. Susan Jeffers. *Feel the Fear and Do it Anyway®*. Vermilion, an imprint of Edbury Press, Random House UK. London: 1987, 2007.

14. James D. Boulgarides; William A. Cohen. Leadership Style vs. Leadership Tactics. *The Journal of Applied Management and Entrepreneurship*: Spring 2001 (Vol. 6, No. 1pp. 59–73).

15. Martha Barletta. Marketing to Women. [Accessed: May 13, 2013.] http://knowledge.wharton.upenn.edu/article/what-women-buy-and-why.

16. Robert Rosenthal; Lenore Jacobson. *Pygmalion in the classroom*. Rinehart and Winston. P. 73. New York: 1968.

17. John Robert Eggen. Teleseminar of The Leading Mentors Publishing and Marketing Program™. The Mission Marketing Mentors, Inc.

18. Jeremy Wright. "Pickle Jar" Theory of Time Management.

19. Helmut von Bialy. Persönlichkeitsentwicklung durch transformatorisches Lernen. (Personality development through transformational learning.) Second online version. Hamburg: July 2006.

20. Burkhard Strassmann. Unglaublich komisch. (Research of Laughing—"Incredibly funny.") http://zeit.de/2011/17/Lachforschung [Accessed: June 13, 2013.] Zeit Online: April 2011.

21. Leslie C. Bell. Hard to Get. http://psychologytoday.com/blog/hard-get/201303/relationship-training-ambitious-20-something-women. [Accessed: August 11, 2013.] *Psychology Today*: March 2013.

22. From *Love the One You're With*, ©2008 Emily Giffin. Reprinted by permission of St. Martin's Press. All rights reserved.

23. From *MAMBO NO. 5 (A LITTLE BIT OF. . .)* by Prado/Bega/Zippy © Promotora Hispano Americana de Musica S.A., Mexico,Reprinted by permission of Peermusic (Germany) GmbH, Hamburg.

Additional Resources

In case you haven't already done; don't forget to download your complimentary *Butterfly Habits Mini Guide, Scout and Planner* to keep you inspired and on track. Visit the following links now to access these three bonus resources and more:

ButterflyHabits.com/mini-guide
ButterflyHabits.com/scout
ButterflyHabits.com/planner

And if you enjoy my philosophy and style stay connected with ButterflyHabits.com for ongoing inspiration, tools and support to make your relationship and life the best it can be.

Are you a smart, professional woman who wants to go beyond this book to deepen and expand her relationship talents? Then you may be interested in my upcoming mentoring program. To learn more about other products and programs visit

FannyRitter.com

Capture Your Butterfly Habits Insights Here

Capture Your Butterfly Habits Insights Here

Butterfly Habits

Capture Your Butterfly Habits Insights Here

About the Author

FANNY RITTER MILZ, lic.rer.pol. is an outstanding Communication and Performance Coach with a Swiss University Master's Degree in Economics and Social Sciences. She enjoyed a highly successful career in HR Recruitment and Placement Services in Zürich/Switzerland, for years. Due to significant changes in her life situation, Fanny decided to pursue studies in neuro-linguistic programming as well as in coaching, where she graduated as "NLP Master Practitioner" and "Certified International NLP Coach." Fanny is member of the Spanish Coaching Association (ASESCO) and the International Coach Federation (ICF). She dedicates her professional expertise as an author, speaker and coach to assisting ambitious women enhance their life quality. Her mission is to help them realize the power of destiny they hold within themselves. After many years of enjoying a fulfilled relationship with her late husband, Fanny is happily married to Urs.

Her motto: Relationships Create Your Future!

Learn more about Fanny at FannyRitter.com